A NEW PEN

Belle and Lilly

Or, the golden rule : a story for girls

A NEW PEN

Belle and Lilly
Or, the golden rule : a story for girls

ISBN/EAN: 9783741192883

Manufactured in Europe, USA, Canada, Australia, Japa

Cover: Foto ©Andreas Hilbeck / pixelio.de

Manufactured and distributed by brebook publishing software (www.brebook.com)

A NEW PEN

Belle and Lilly

BELLE AND LILLY:

OR,

THE GOLDEN RULE.

A

STORY FOR GIRLS.

BY

A NEW PEN.

EMBELLISHED WITH SIX COLORED ENGRAVINGS.

NEW YORK:
P. O'SHEA, PUBLISHER,
27 BARCLAY STREET.

Entered according to Act of Congress, in the year 1867,

By P. O'SHEA,

In the Clerk's Office of the District Court of the United States, for the Southern District of New York.

CONTENTS.

CHAPTER I.
THE ARRIVAL 1

CHAPTER II.
THE CHILDREN'S PARTY 13

CHAPTER III.
SICKNESS 31

CHAPTER IV.
SCHOOL DAYS 56

CHAPTER V.
THE LAST DAY OF THE QUARTER . . . 86

CHAPTER VI.
THE OLD FARM AND ITS INMATES . . 112

CHAPTER VII.
COUNTRY LIFE 123

CHAPTER VIII.
THE PICNIC 157

CHAPTER I.

THE ARRIVAL.

"Do, my own dear, sweet mamma, let me put on my new dress, and my gold bracelet and locket, this afternoon, for you know Cousin Belle is coming, and Uncle Harley is rich, so she will be all dressed up, and I want to look nice too; won't you, mamma dear?"

"Yes, yes, Lilly, go away and tell Katie to put on just what you want, and don't come to me again for two hours at least, for I am very busy."

Lilly ran away, delighted, — scarcely waiting to hear anything but the yes, yes, and was out of sight in a moment. The seeds of vanity and folly were already deeply sown in this child's heart, — seeds that, if not uprooted soon, would spring up and bear abundant fruit, —

fruit which would cause sorrow and anguish, which would turn her beauty into ugliness, and make it far better for her had she been born deformed, and in the midst of poverty.

Mrs. Mordaunt was a young, thoughtless, and pretty woman, good-hearted and merry, but without any fixed and guiding principle,— contented to glide along life as easily as possible and to get all the enjoyment she could with little trouble, doing no one any good, and, she thought, no one any harm. At the time we introduced her to you, she was reading a novel, just in the most interesting part, and did not wish to be interrupted. We will leave her and follow her young daughter.

She ran quietly along until she came to her mother's chamber; there she found Katie busily engaged cleaning.

"Katie, Katie, come right away and dress me," imperiously cries the little despot. "I am to have on my new silk, my bracelet, my necklace, and my locket, and you must come right away and get them for me,— ma says so."

"Indeed, Miss Lilly, I cannot come quite yet, for I am just in the midst of my work, and I can't leave the things all helter-skelter. Your ma told me to clean her room, and you must wait."

"But I sha'n't wait, Miss Katie, and I will go right off and tell mamma you won't come when she said you must; and then you shall go away from here — so — you ugly girl."

"Well, go," Katie replied, in a careless tone, "I can't leave this dirt in the middle of the floor, and I sha'n't either, unless mistress orders it herself."

Away went Lilly, and with loud complaints against Katie interrupted her mother again.

Mrs. Mordaunt was now obliged to put by her book and listen to the affair.

"What was Katie doing, Lilly?"

"O, she was sweeping, I believe, and she wouldn't leave it, to come when I called her, — the bad, bad girl!"

The mother laughed, instead of reproving, — laughed at the consequential air of this little six-years-old autocrat, and at her queenly carriage.

"Well, well, Lilly dear, you must wait awhile, for I remember I told Katie to clean my room thoroughly to-day; so sit down and look at these pictures and eat some candy, and by and by you shall be attended to."

Lilly was satisfied with the books and candy, and contrived to wait quite patiently for a half-hour, and then her mother told her she might go and see if Katie had finished.

She had,—and readily took Lilly to perform the important task.

And now, all dressed, she danced into the library again to show herself to her mother.

She did indeed look very lovely in her delicate blue silk, with that shower of golden ringlets waving about her snowy neck,—and *she* thought so too, for a smile of satisfaction rested on her little face, as she cried, "See, mamma, — don't I look nice?"

"Lovely, sweet,—you darling little angel!" These were the mother's exclamations, as she turned her around, gazing with admiring pride, — not one glance of which was lost by those bright, quick eyes. "And now, Lilly, it is a whole hour before your cousin comes, — you must keep yourself nice, and don't romp about."

Lilly was very content to sit still, now she was dressed, and play with her doll and baby things, for she wished to surprise her cousin with her fine appearance.

The cousin she was expecting had lost her mother a few months before, and her father sent her to his sister's to go to school, and because, being exceedingly delicate, he thought change of air might benefit her. He had other motives also, which will appear in the course of my story.

"There she is, — there is the carriage, dear mamma. May I go to the door?"

Away she ran without waiting for an answer, and soon returned leading in a pale, shy, and rather plain little girl, dressed very neatly, and with no adornment save an exquisite little bunch of flowers in her hand; her hair was wavy and her eyes large, dark, and spiritual-looking,—you felt at a glance she was lovable, and yet could scarce tell why.

Lilly was excessively disappointed; all her finery had no effect upon her cousin, who never noticed it, apparently; she looked sad and lonely, and scarcely spoke at all.

Mrs. Mordaunt, supposing she was afraid of her, sent them both to the play-room to amuse themselves. We will follow and listen.

"How still you are, Belle," says Lilly; "are you sorry that I have got a silk dress, and a bracelet, and locket, and you not any? I would give you some like these if I had any more."

Belle smiled faintly as she said, "O no, Lilly, I don't care for that; but you know I have no mother now, and I have left my dear father, and little Willie, and I am all alone here." And the tears began to fill her eyes.

Little Lilly did not know what to do. Never having seen any one in real distress, she did not quite understand what to make of it; but she was an affectionate child, so she threw her arms around her cousin's neck and kissed her, and begged her not to cry.

This was the best thing she could have done, and Belle was comforted. Soon she and Lilly were busily engaged in their play-house. All Lilly cared for was dressing and undressing the dollys; but Belle tried to teach her to play with them, and pretend they understood, and were real children. Belle was three years older than Lilly, so she could teach her very well.

While they were thus engaged, another little one had crept in, gone softly up to the play-house, and snatched out one of the largest dolls and ran away in high glee.

"I will take her a riding in my cart, Lilly, — you come and see," said Harry, holding it high above his head.

"I won't, Harry, you ugly, naughty boy; you sha'n't have my dolly. I will go and tell mother."

She ran, and Harry ran. He fell, and dashed the doll all to pieces in his fall. Lilly caught up to him, slapped him in the face as he lay kicking on the floor, and ran screaming to her mother, with the broken doll in her hand.

Belle looked on, shocked and stupefied. Soon, however, she recovered her senses, and went up to the little boy, who was crying hard and had not arisen.

"Don't come here," he cried, "don't come

here. You are a girl, and just like Lill. I *hate* girls, so go away."

"But Harry, Cousin Harry, won't you let me help you up, and brush the dust off from you, and bathe your poor head, where it is all swollen and black? I will not hurt you."

Surprised by her gentle tones, he looked up and said, "Then you don't like Lill, and you will go with me, and you are not ugly and cross as she is?"

"O, don't talk so, Harry dear. I *do* like Lilly and you too. I love you both, and you must love us both."

"No, no, I sha'n't, Belle. I will not like Lilly, for she never lets me play with her, nor look at her baby-house and playthings, and so I will always plague her and run away with any of them whenever I get a chance."

"O Harry," said Belle, with her eyes full of tears, and a face of sadness, "is that doing as you would be done by? Mamma, my dear mamma, used to tell me that I must be good to *every one*, even if they were not good to me; that if it made me feel badly to be treated unkindly, I might know it would another, and —"

"Dear! dear! what are you talking about, Belle? I never heard such — I don't know what ever you mean. You are good, and I love and will kiss you; and all that talk about doing and being good to people that are cross to me, I don't understand; but I will listen to you some other time. Now I am going to smash the baby-house to pay Lill for my bruises." And away he ran.

"Don't! don't! O pray, don't!" imploringly cried Belle, running after him and seizing his hand, and then looking earnestly into his face with her sweet eyes. "Don't you love Belle a little, — just a wee bit?"

"Yes, yes, a great deal, — of course I do; but let me go."

"Then for my sake stop, — let Lilly's baby-house alone and come with me. I will tell you a better way to treat Lilly, and a way that will make you happier too."

She was so eager that Harry consented at last, and went off with his little cousin.

Lilly had by this time made all her complaints to her mother, who promised her a new doll, and pacified her in various ways, calling

Harry a naughty boy, without inquiring at all into the merits of the case; and thus Lilly was made unconscious of her own faults, but fully alive to those of others. She stayed awhile with her mother, played with her jewel-box, and decorated herself before the glass with its contents; and when tired of that, took them off again, and dropped the box and contents on the floor, and ran off to find Belle.

Upon entering the play-room, what was her astonishment to find Harry and Belle there, and both so busily engaged they did not hear her enter. She crept softly along to see what they were about, ready to be angry with both, for she supposed of course they were in mischief. But her eyes rested upon a beautiful new wax dolly in Belle's hands, who was hastily and busily dressing it in some of the broken doll's clothes, while Harry was employed in arranging the disorderly baby-house. Every now and then, he would ask Belle if he was putting things right.

"How pleased Lill will be, Belle! I am so glad I spent my dollar for the doll, for I have broken lots of Lilly's playthings, and I always thought it was good fun; but I think this fun is the best after all, for Lill will be so surprised, and may be she will let me play with her more now. It was all you, Belle. I never should have thought of such a way to act. Nobody ever said such things to me before."

"O Harry, how pretty she is! See!" and she held her up. "She is all dressed; aint she pretty?"

Lilly made a sudden movement,—they both looked around and saw her close beside them, and knew she must have heard all that had been said. Lilly gazed first at one and then at the other in mute surprise, then seized the dolly and kissed it again and again, and then hugged Harry and Belle. At last came her words: "Harry, I am sorry I told mother you were ugly, for you are not now; and I am so sorry I pushed you down, and made that great bruise on your head. I will not be so cross any more." And she kissed him.

Harry was a warm-hearted boy, easily moved and easily subdued. He had never seen Lilly so affectionate before, and he was ready to love her at once.

"Never mind, Lilly, I was cross too. I will try not to be so any more. Perhaps I shall love you as well as Belle, some time."

Lilly was rather mortified by his last speech. However, she managed to keep from showing it, and the three amused themselves very pleasantly together for the rest of the afternoon. Harry brought in his games and rocking-horse, and they had fine play.

Thus passed the first half-day of Cousin Belle at her new home.

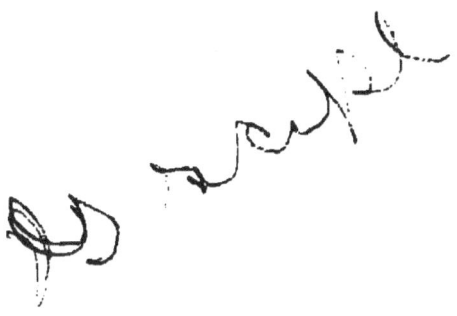

CHAPTER II.

THE CHILDREN'S PARTY.

BELLE had been about six months at her uncle's, and was quite reconciled to her new abode. Little Harry and she were great friends; and from intercourse with his cousin he had become very gentle and unselfish.

But Lilly, although often by impulse pleasant and affectionate, was too vain and regardless of others, naturally, to alter a great deal so soon; but she loved her cousin Belle dearly, and would yield for her sooner than for any one else

One day, she came running into the room, her face radiant with delight: "O Belle! to-morrow is my birthday, and mamma says I may have a little party. Only think, I am seven years old," — and she stretched herself up on tiptoe to appear as tall as possible, — "and mamma says I may have twenty little girls and boys to come to tea; so, Harry and Belle, help me think who we shall invite."

Harry clapped his hands and ran dancing about the room for joy; and Belle's eyes sparkled at the prospect of so much pleasure. "O, is n't it nice! what a grand time we will have!"

"Yes," said Harry, "won't we? I hope you will invite some of the *little* boys, — Tom Gillmore and Willie Wilson, — for *I* love them, and we can have fun together."

"No, no, Harry! they are only five years old, and nothing but babies, and I only want those that can dance."

Harry looked disappointed. "Why, *I* am not a baby, Lill, and they are just as old as me; but I suppose you don't want *me* in the room"; and he turned away with his lip just ready to cry.

"Now don't *be a baby*," said Lilly, "or I am sure I sha'n't want you. Just to please *you*, I believe I will have Tommy and Willie, so don't be cross."

BELLE AND LILLY. 15

Harry cheered up at once, and went and kissed his unusually good-natured sister, which kiss she received as grandly as if she were a little queen.

"Well, Belle, who shall we invite? You have n't said a word, and yet you looked pleased when I told you."

"I am pleased, dear Lilly, and more pleased now than I was then, because you have been so good to Harry. I suppose you will invite all the girls you know very well, and that will not be more than twenty."

"O no!" said Lilly; "I don't want Bessie Landon, for she pushed me down at school the other day; and I don't want Sallie Sheldon, for she is so selfish she never will play nicely; and I don't want Letty Lee, for she is so poor, and dresses so badly, I hate to look at her; and I —"

"O Lilly, Lilly! do stop," said Belle. "You are running on so fast, by and by you will have no one left to invite. If you leave out every one that does not happen to suit you, or that has a fault, there won't be many left; and not to invite a girl because she happens to be poor — how unkind! Only think, Lilly, if you or I were poor, it would not be our fault; and then think how much she would enjoy it, for she does not have many pleasures, and she is such a merry little thing."

"O, well let's invite *her* then, but not the others. I aint a going to have them."

"O do Lilly dear! do have them all, for you know *we* would not like to be left out because we had some fault or other which somebody did n't like. I know you will enjoy yourself better, to invite all the girls that you know intimately, without regard to their faults."

"Well then, to please you, I will invite all my class, and some in the other older classes; and now, 'am I doing as I would be done by?' for I suppose you will be saying that to me before long, — you always are, — and I don't see why you should; no one else does."

"Perhaps I do tease you sometimes, dear Lilly, but those words are ever in my mind; they were almost the last my dying mother said to me, and her pale face and gentle voice impress them upon my heart, and I think sometimes I can hear her saying them to me,— I feel her hand upon my head, and her soft kiss on my cheek; that is why I say them so often. But I hope I don't plague you with my sermons, as you call them."

"O no, Belle dear! but I do like to please myself, and not be always thinking of others, and you, it seems to me, never think of yourself until the last. I wonder if *I* shall be as good in three years! I don't believe it, but may be so. But come now, don't let us stand talking any longer, for we must go and invite."

Away they went, as happy as bright young hearts could be, and soon the little folks were bidden, and Belle and Lilly back again, as rosy and fresh as a nice brisk walk in the cold air could make them.

Lilly was quite excited, and could talk of nothing but the party, and what they should do to amuse themselves, and what they should wear. Mrs. Mordaunt promised to play for them to dance, and they were to have the play-room, for all kind of games. Before the two little girls closed their eyes that night, all the plans were arranged for the morrow, and a fine time was anticipated.

They found it hard to go to school the next morning, and attend to their lessons. Lilly's little head was full of the party, and her lessons were very imperfect, and even Belle missed. At intermission nothing else was talked of, and all the girls clustered around Belle and Lilly, to ask questions and to rejoice.

Miss Millar, the teacher, soon found out what was in the wind, and then she did not much wonder at the imperfect lessons. If mothers will be foolish enough to let their children have parties, they can't expect them to study at the same time.

As soon as school was over, they hastened home and as hastily swallowed their dinners, eager to begin to dress for the occasion.

Lilly had improved much in the last four or five months; there was a gentle, kind, sweet look in her face often now, and she was so very pretty, that, with the expression of amiability added to her other charms, she made a picture few could pass without a second look.

Now, in her light blue merino dress, neck and arms bare, and sleeves looped up with coral, and a coral necklace on her soft white throat, her beautiful golden curls falling in such rich profusion, shading her rosy cheeks, and her eyes sparkling with pleasure, she was indeed a little vision of delight.

Belle, too, was very lovely; although not as regularly beautiful as Lilly, there was an angelic expression in those dark eyes, and a sweetness playing in the dimples about her small red lips, that was very bewitching; she was dressed like Lilly exactly, — except she had a rose-bud and some heliotrope put among the dark clusters of her hair.

She had improved also since she came to her uncle's; being in better health, her cheeks wore more of the rose hue, and her figure was more plump and round; the sadness which then seemed the prevailing expression of her face had now disappeared, and she looked bright and happy.

The little guests have all arrived, I believe not one absentee. Even Lottie Lee, with her best mousselin-de-laine on, was there; and although it was coarse and dark-colored, yet her brown curls looked pretty on her bare neck, and her bright black eyes danced just as happily as if she had been dressed in silk. Belle welcomed her, even more cordially than any one, kissing her brown cheek and putting her arm around her fat little waist.

Boys and girls all proceeded to the playroom, a large and sunny one, on the southern side of the house. Here were all the thousand and one toys which Lilly, Belle, and Harry had collected. There they had a fine romp, — tag, hunt the slipper, blind man's buff, all followed each other in quick succession. All was harmony and peace, and not a quarrel was heard. Mirth and joy seemed to reign in every heart.

When tea was ready, they were all tired out, and quite willing to sit still and rest awhile. All the little folks sat around a long table, which was loaded with an abundance of good things, to which they did ample justice. Then the drawing-rooms were lighted up, and Mrs. Mordaunt invited them all in there to dance, until time for departure. The parents came in the evening, and were quite delighted in watching the pleasures of their darlings.

Now let us amuse ourselves, watching and listening. See Belle in the dance with that noble-looking boy; how light her step, and how joyous her glance. She has a smile for all, and how lovely that smile is. Lilly is in the same set; she does not know, or else does not choose to recollect, that as hostess she should see that all her little guests were amused before she enjoyed herself. She was very fond of dancing, and certainly appeared like a little fairy when she did dance; her very soul was in it; her cheeks rosy with excitement, and her eyes and whole face lighted with animation.

I presume she does not imagine that every one is not as happy as herself, and does not notice the two in the corner looking so discontented and unhappy; they are evidently helping each other on in their sad feelings. We will join the group ere long. Not far from them are three or four others busily engaged in some game which seems to excite great laughter; the parents and relatives, a few of whom were invited with the children, are looking on with much pleasure, greatly amused by the sight. Mrs. Mordaunt is playing for the dances. And now you are introduced to the guests, let us listen to the talk of the two we spoke about, Julia Talbot and Alice Edmonds.

"I don't see why it is, Julia, everybody likes that Belle Harley so much. She is n't pretty a bit; and so stuck up. The boys all run after her, as well as the girls. There, Edgar Morris came right by *you* and asked *her* to dance, and so did Harry Page."

"And you too, Alice; they passed you too." And she cast a glance of dislike upon poor Belle.

"I know that, Julia; but then you are prettier than I am, and certainly as pretty as Belle, and dressed much handsomer."

"O well, Alice, I dare say they thought they must ask her first, and then may be they did not notice us; but I never did like Belle any way, — she pretends so much goodness."

The girls were so busy talking that they did not notice the dancers had changed their position, and Belle Harley had been quite near them for some minutes. Alice had been entertaining Julia with various anecdotes of Belle's saintship, and of her always trying to make others appear wrong, &c., when suddenly Julia looked up with, "O dear! I wish she had stayed at home with her father." Her eye caught Belle's, who had heard the whole, and who was gazing at her with a sad look and tears on her cheek.

"O Alice," Julia whispered, "there is Belle, and she has heard every word we have said, and I am so sorry; I don't believe she is so hateful, for she don't look *angry* at all."

"Very well," said Alice; "I am willing she should hear. I have only said what I thought. She knows I don't like her; I have taken no pains to conceal it." But here she comes, so I will leave you—"

"O don't, Alice, don't leave me just now!" But she was off like a flash; and Julia, blushing and confused, had not a word to say.

"I thought you were both dancing, Julia," Belle said, in a sweet, winning voice, "until I happened to come near you a short time ago.

Now do take my place, dear, won't you? for I am quite tired." And she looked at her partner, who of course asked Julia if he might have the pleasure.

Julia, surprised and altogether confused by this pleasant manner, knowing how little she deserved it, was about to say something and decline; but Belle had gone before she recovered her senses, and Edgar led her to the dance.

The next thing, Julia saw Belle leading a fine-looking boy up to Alice to introduce her, and soon Alice and herself were dancing in the same set, where they forgot their ill-will, and perhaps were ashamed of it.

Julia danced with great animation; but in the midst of a figure a clumsy boy, who nearly fell, caught hold of her dress and tore a long rent. She was almost pulled over, and, in the effort to save herself, broke her bracelet, the beads of which scattered in every direction upon the floor.

Julia was much distressed. Belle was among the first by her side to help. She left the game she was engaged in and ran to her, found many of the beads, and then took her to another room to mend her dress for her, first substituting another in her place for the dance.

Julia, who was in reality very tenderhearted, could not help being touched by such undeserved kindness, for she had ever treated Belle coldly, and kept her at a distance. Now she said to her:—

"Why, Belle, how can you treat me so kindly, and what makes you so affectionate? I always thought you cold and proud, and not caring for any of us, because we were not good, and you heard me talking about you, and saying ugly things, and yet you leave all your enjoyment to come and help me, now I am in trouble; I am sure *I* would have been *glad*, to see any one *I* disliked in trouble, but your plan is best, dear Belle, for you have taken all the bad feelings I had against you from my heart, and made me long to be like you; a little while ago I felt as if I hated you."

Belle smiled, and threw her arms around the excited girl's neck, softly whispering, "You will never feel so again, will you, Julia? I dare say I may have seemed cold and reserved to you and many of the girls, for I have been sad and thinking all about myself; so I did not look around me, and see how I could help others enjoy, or care what others thought about me, — that was selfish, and I hope I shall act differently in future."

The girls went back hand in hand, and Julia Talbot was ever, after this, the firm upholder of Belle Harley and her sworn friend upon all occasions.

When they entered the parlor, the children were all busily engaged in eating ice-cream, candy, nuts, and cake, which were provided in abundance. Belle and Julia soon joined in the occupation; how unwise in Mrs. Mordaunt, merely to indulge a love for show, to put such a variety before these young people,— for of course none, unless they were prevented by the older ones, would abstain; so their little stomachs were crowded with all those unwholesome things.

Belle and Lilly were very delicate children, yet they were not restricted; and, knowing no better, they ate too great a variety of the tempting eatables. The consequences may be foreseen. After supper, the little folks had another dance, and then their mammas thought it high time for them to depart; so with evident reluctance they bid good night, expressing most rapturously their delight in the party, and hoping some one else would have a birthday soon.

Julia and Alice walked home together. Julia could talk only of Belle.

"O, Alice," she said, "I said a great many ugly things about Belle to-night, and *have* often; I am so ashamed of them all, for I love her *now* and always *shall*, and only wish *I* were, or *could* be, half as good."

"'Hem!'" said Alice, mockingly, "you have changed very suddenly, to be sure; *you* can like her if you choose, and everybody else can, but *I* never will; she is always looking upon me with scorn, and setting up her superior goodness, and I hate to be with her,—she is not one bit like the other girls."

"That is, because other girls aint half as good as she is, and so her presence is a kind of reproach to them and makes them feel uncomfortable."

"Ah indeed! and since when has Miss Julia Talbot became so good as to *enjoy* the company of the little saint, — about two hours ago you were railing at her."

"I know it, Alice, I know it, and I am so sorry. O Alice, I did not mean to say I was any better than you, for I used to feel just so, but if you could only have been with us, when she was so gentle and kind to me, who had just been abusing her; if you could only have seen her sad face, and her eyes full of tears when she spoke of her dear mother, and have felt her loving kiss after she had been doing a service to you, — especially if you, like me, had never been anything but ugly to her, — I am sure your heart would have warmed to her as mine has, and you would be sorry that you had ever felt as you do."

"Well, may be she is a saint or an angel; but I don't like her, and never shall."

"Don't, Alice, pray don't say that, — I am sure you will repent it."

Alice laughed, as she said, "Good night, I

am home now! I hope in your new love for Belle you will not give up old friends, Julia dear, for I love *you* dearly if I don't her." So saying, with a kiss they parted.

Let us stop a moment to speak of Alice. She was a thoughtless, selfish, and rather domineering young girl; but, my young friends, she had no mother. When she was an infant that tender-loving parent had been taken away, leaving her and her brother Alfred with their father, a man absorbed in business life, and *he* thought if they were only well fed, well clothed, and sent to school, that all that was necessary had been done. The training of the immortal soul was never in his mind. I doubt whether he ever remembered that he or they had souls, or that it ever occurred to him there was any pursuit in life so important as money-making. He brought to his house, after his wife's death, a sister of his own, their maiden aunt, just as worldly as himself. Her system of education was strict, to be sure; but the law of love formed no part of its element. She seldom looked into the motives for action, and judged accordingly. If they were noisy or cross or meddlesome or impudent, they would be shut up or whipped. Thus their finer feelings were blunted, and their moral nature warped and deformed. So let us pity more than blame Alice; the envy and malice which filled her breast harmed herself, but could not harm the object that caused it. So it is ever, — our evil passions turn back upon our own souls. "They are like chickens, ever coming home to roost."

Both the children had noble qualities, and one redeeming trait was their affection for each other. Some power may yet be sent to touch their hearts, and bring forth into action that virtue and goodness which now lie dormant.

CHAPTER III.

SICKNESS.

THE party with all its bright anticipations was over; the morning sun rose gloriously the next day, but many hours had he been in the sky ere our little friends opened their eyes to his light.

Belle was up, and dressed, her morning prayers over, and still Lilly moved not, save every now and then she would toss, and turn, and moan, in her restless slumber. At last Belle went softly to her bed to look at her. She was so pale, and dark under her eyes, that Belle was frightened.

"Lilly, Lilly dear, are you sick?" she whispered.

Lilly opened her eyes languidly and tried to speak, but she only muttered something not intelligible; so Belle ran quickly and called Katy, who was in the next room. Katy came, gave one look, and started hastily off again in search of her mother.

By this time Lilly, instead of being pale, had a crimson spot on each cheek, and her eyes were opened wide and staring.

Mrs. Mordaunt was terribly alarmed, and, as usual, lost all presence of mind. She wrung her hands, and cried, and moaned, exciting still more the nervous irritability of her child.

Belle left the room at once and despatched a servant for the Doctor. In the mean time Mrs. Mordaunt was pacing backwards and forwards, and raving that her "Lilly, her idol, would die."

"Auntie, auntie," said Belle, going quietly up to her and placing her small hand in hers, "had you not better sit down still beside Lilly and bathe her head? don't you see how her eyes follow you, and how restless it makes her?"

Her attention thus called to it, Mrs. Mordaunt aroused her faculties and really became useful. She seated herself by her little daughter, sent Katie for ice-water and Belle for a sponge, and calmed herself as well as Lilly.

In a half-hour Doctor Rossitur was by her bedside. He was a man of most excellent sense, able, firm, and energetic, and was moreover a friend as well as physician.

He gave one glance at Lilly, felt her pulse and head, then said: "Your daughter has the scarlet fever, madam! It is prevalent. But the symptoms are accelerated and aggravated by an undigested mass upon the stomach. Has she been eating improper food lately?"

"She may have taken too much ice-cream last night, and too much cake, and perhaps nuts and raisins."

"Mrs. Mordaunt," said the Doctor, slowly and sternly, "are you a sensible woman and a mother, and do you not know that no grown person, much less a child of seven years, should take such a mess as that into their stomachs? If she recover from this, I will only say she has a strong constitution, and—" But seeing the look of terror and anguish upon the face of Mrs. Mordaunt, he ceased, and soothingly added, "but be comforted, madam, it is her first sickness; I will do my best, and she will have good nursing, so I trust all will be well; but take this as a warning and a lesson, and learn how to regulate your child's appetite in future."

Then turning to Belle, who stood pale and tearful by the bedside: "You had better not be here, child; you will be sick next. Did you, too, eat *only nuts, and raisins, and cake, and ice-cream?*"

Belle blushed and hung her head, as she replied, "Yes, Doctor, I ate some of those things, but not a great deal, and *I* do not feel very well to-day."

The Doctor looked at her attentively, and after feeling her pulse told her he would write her a prescription, which she must take faithfully and not leave her room again that day, and on no account to come near Lilly until he told her she could do so with safety.

So Belle had to go most reluctantly to her own room, and *there* she had to stay for a week, feeling wretchedly, and *all* in consequence of eating improperly. During this whole week Lilly raved incessantly, her life hung by a thread; and poor Mrs. Mordaunt, the picture of misery, hung over her couch night and day. Katie, too, was a faithful nurse.

At the end of the week the child sunk into a profound slumber. What a relief to the watchers to see the poor disturbed child at rest! to see a sweet, placid expression upon the still, pale face, instead of the wild, distorted look and rolling eyes!

Mrs. Mordaunt threw herself upon the couch in the room, and slept soundly, too.

When the doctor came in the morning Lilly was still sleeping, but Mrs. Mordaunt was bending over her in agony,—"My child is dead, she is dead!"—and she fell back, fainting.

The doctor seized a glass and placed it before her lips, for he felt no pulse; a faint breath suffused the glass. "She lives!" he cried, "and will probably arouse out of this slumber better; if her senses are returned when she awakes she will recover. Let there be no noise, not a sound to disturb her; let nature take its course. Katie, take care of

Mrs. Mordaunt; I will watch beside Lilly, to-day."

Twelve hours longer she slept. The doctor kept his watch, excluding all others from the room. He held one hand; he felt the fingers move; he looked in her face, her eyelids were unclosing, and a very faint tinge came upon her cheek and lips. Now a sound escapes. Ah, how he listens for the word! how much depends upon that awakening!

"Mamma, where am I? where have I been?"

"Lilly, child, you have been sick, but keep still, you are better now."

"You here, doctor, I want mamma, and Belle."

"Well, well, child, don't talk now, and they will soon come. Thank God, thank God, she will get well!" — and the good doctor wiped his eyes, as he turned from the bed and got up to call the mother.

I will not describe the mother's joy, — all can imagine that; from this day, Lilly slowly recovered Belle had regained her usual health and was permitted to come again into the sick room, where she loved to be; and, although only ten years old, she was an able assistant, for the spirit was willing, the love was in her heart; this it was which made her hands active, and her sweet voice always tender and gentle. Lilly was a very restive, sick child, having always been indulged during her short life; she could not understand now the necessity of being denied all the good things she wanted, and she rebelled terribly against the nauseous doses she was compelled to swallow. As she grew better and strong, the more impatient and fretful she became, and even her indulgent mother found her very troublesome. Belle alone could influence her, and Belle she could not bear out of her sight; she forgot in her selfishness that any one else could be weary.

One day during the third or fourth week of her illness, Mrs. Mordaunt left her with Belle for an hour or two, leaving directions with Katie to attend to them.

"Shall I read aloud to you, Lilly? I have just found a very pretty little story in my new book that father sent me, would you like to hear it?"

"I don't know, read a little and I'll see; if it is all about religion I don't want to hear it; begin it, and if I don't like it I'll tell you."

Although the assent was rather ungracious, Belle commenced, for she felt sure she could amuse her little cousin better by it than in any other way.

The story was about one of the poor little match sellers that frequent the streets of our large cities. A little girl only five or six years old was sent out by a drunken mother every day to get a few pence, which were ever appropriated to her own vile uses. If the poor child failed in her mission she had to get a beating; it was a very sad story, and both the children were in tears over it soon.

"O," said Lilly, "I wish I had been there! I would have pinched and scratched that wicked woman, and I would have run away if she had been my mother; I never would have spoke to her again."

"But, Lilly, may be she had been good to her sometime; besides, that would n't have been the way to make her better, by being bad yourself, and she must have been so unhappy, the poor, wicked woman."

"Well, she had no need to have been so wicked; I don't see why you pity her."

"Are we always good, Lilly? and we don't have half as much to make us bad as the poor, poor people have. I have heard papa say, that if we who thought ourselves so pure and righteous had one third of the temptations that the low poor have, we might not be any better, if as good."

"Well, well, you talk just like a teacher, Belle; but go on, I wait to hear the rest!"

Belle continued reading. "One day she went out when it was very cold, the snow was on the ground, and the frost in the air; the sleighs were gliding merrily along with their gay burdens; beautiful women and sweet little girls and boys were daintily treading the streets, dressed in furs, and velvet, and lace, and satin. Men, with their warm cloaks and coats, and all of their faces covered up but the tips of their noses, passed unheedingly by, when this poor little solitary being of six years crept along with her bare toes, and thin, ragged dress, old shawl, and dirty, tattered straw bonnet, crying, 'Matches, matches to sell, who'll buy?' Her voice was sweet and gentle, though weak and low; her face was very pretty, except it was so pale and so sad-looking and *so thin*. Not far had she travelled ere her lips refused to speak at her bidding, they were so stiff and cold; she tried and tried, but not a loud word could she utter; then the tears ran down her cheeks and froze as they fell upon her dress; still she went on and on, until her *feet*, too, became stiff and numb; then, no longer able to move, she seated herself upon a door-step, and burying her face in her lap sobbed as if her heart would break: 'O dear! O dear! what shall I do? I have sold no matches and I can't go any further, and if I go home I shall get a beating. O dear! O dear! if I could only die!'" Here Belle's voice failed her, and both of them sobbed aloud.

"Poor little girl!" said Lilly, as soon as she could speak, "that is a great deal worse than being sick as I have been, although I have had to have so much pain and take so much medicine."

"O yes, Lilly, a great deal worse, for you had those around you who loved you all the time, and heard only affectionate words and saw only kind looks."

"But yet I have been cross and impatient, and sometimes real ugly to dear mamma, and so peevish and fretful to you. O dear! O dear! how hard it is to be good; how I wish I could be!"

"I am sure you will be, dear Lilly," said Belle, soothingly, "if you wish it so much. But it *is* hard, very hard; and we have to try so long. It is so much easier to be naughty I sometimes think."

"Do you?" said Lilly; "do *you* ever have to *try* to be good? I thought you did not know how to be bad, and that you were not at all like other children; for all I knew were sometimes naughty, but *you*, never!"

Belle blushed at such undeserved praise, as she thought, and replied very earnestly, "O Lilly, how can you talk so, when you have heard me so often speak cross, and have seen my selfishness. You have forgotten about the drawing and the book, I guess; but no one knows how much I struggle with myself, or how I long to be what dear mother was."

"The book and the drawing, Belle! what do you mean? O, I remember! when Harry spoiled your drawing you called him a clumsy fellow, and wished he would learn to take a little care, &c.; and I would like to know who would n't have said as much and more; spoiling your beautiful picture that you had been so long finishing, and —"

"But it was my own fault, Lilly. I should not have left it about; and besides, even if it had not been, it did no good to make little Harry feel badly. It did not better the picture."

"Well, I don't care, we can't be quite like saints. But what about the book? you have never been cross about any book that I know of."

"No! not exactly cross, but selfish; for I wanted the handsomest, and seized upon it first when asked to take my choice."

"Well, and so you should, for papa meant the handsomest for you; for you had had no New Year's present from him, and I had one or two."

"Well, dear Lilly, excuse me as much as

you will, it shows how much you love me; yet still you cannot convince me that I was not selfish and cross, and am so far oftener than I ought to be. And now let's read on; don't you say so?"

"Yes, yes, do, for I suppose you will think as you please in spite of what everybody else says, and I want to hear what became of the poor little girl." So Belle read on.

"There she sat sobbing, and not raising her head from her hands, until gradually she seemed to get all over stiff, and aching in every limb. She could not move. People passed and repassed, saw her sitting there but were too busy about their own matters to heed. Now a gentle drowsiness was creeping upon her, and she began to feel so happy her head fell over on her shoulder; and her face had such a seraphic expression, it surely seemed as if angels were ministering to her. Suddenly a sweet voice seemed to whisper in her ear. Its tones were so gentle and the words so kind, that the little girl thought she had really gone to that heaven she used to hear about when her mother was kind to her, — so she did not open her eyes, and she could not speak again.

"'My poor little child, what are you sitting here on these icy steps for? What do you want? Come in, come in with me.'

"Then there was a little, gentle shake, but still no answer; only the large dark eyes slowly unclosed and gazed for an instant on the beautiful, kind face bending over her, and then closed again, while her lips murmured, 'It is an angel, and I am in heaven!' then again she sunk back more lethargic than ever. Then she was taken softly up and carried into a large, splendid house, and laid upon a soft bed in a cold room, and rubbed with snow and with the hands until the warmth began again to return to the poor, thin limbs, and the color to the faded lips and cheeks. Every care and attention she had, and her young spirit was brought back again to earth; near to heaven it certainly had been, for a few minutes longer and no care or help could have restored her; and perhaps you will say far better had it been for the sorrowing child had she been left to depart; but God had a work for this little one to perform, — 'His ways are not as our ways.' Let us never question his wisdom, even when all seems dark to us.

"The lady (would there were many such good Samaritans) had her washed and dressed neatly and warmly, and then, when she was able, asked to hear her story.

"A lovely little fairy of about her own age came bounding into the room just as Nora was commencing.

"'O mother, mother! do let the little girl stay here and be my little sister; I have none, and it will be so nice to have her to play with. You will stay, won't you?' and with her own little delicate hand she took hold of the swollen red fingers of the little beggar child; 'tell me your name right away, and let 's go off and play.'

"The lady was silent, — she wished to hear the child answer.

"'O thank you, thank you! dear little lady,' said the pale, forlorn one; 'why is it every one is so good to me? I was so wretched a little while ago, and thought the world so ugly, and wanted to get away, — now I feel so happy.'

"The little Edith stared as if she thought it very queer what the child was saying, then rushing up to her again, rather impatiently said: 'Why don't you come? and why don't you tell me your name?'

"'My name is Nora, ma'am, but I can't stay here, indeed I can't, although everything is so beautiful, and you all so good. I must go home to my mamma, for she is sick, and I have two little sisters there, and who would take care of them if not me? but, O dear, dear! I hope mother will not beat me this time if I haven't sold any matches!' and she looked around the room rather alarmed, for she missed her basket. 'My basket, my basket! O, where is it?' she cried in agony.

"'O, never mind your basket, child, it was left on the steps, I believe, and before now it will be gone; but you shall have a new one, and have it well filled with things to sell better than matches; but if your mother is so cross to you, Nora, I should think you would be glad to get away from her.'

"'But she isn't always cross; sometimes she seems to love me, and cries over me and little sisters, and hugs us, and says she wishes we were all dead together; and when she is getting well from her dreadful fits she is very good to us If she would only not drink what she makes me get for her in a bottle whenever she has any money, I think she would never be cruel to us.'

"'Poor child, poor child,' said the lady, 'I see how it is; the old story, rum and its consequences. I will take you home, and try if we cannot persuade your mother to be reasonable.'

"'And so Nora is a going, and I am not to have any little playmate after all.' And little Edith put up her little rosy lip very much as if she would cry; but her mamma patted her little curly head and said to her: "Go tell Rosy to put on your coat and hat, darling, and you shall go with Nora and mamma to poor little Nora's home." She ran off speedily, and soon returned, equipped.

"What a contrast the two children afforded. Edith, with her fair rosy face and dimpled cheeks,— her beautiful golden curls hanging around in rich profusion, and her bright, laughing blue eyes.

"Nora, with her pale, sunken cheeks, her large, heavy black eyes, so full of sorrow and patience, her hair in tangled masses and very dark, and her clothes so scanty; although the lady had had her cleanly attired, and a thick plaid shawl nearly covered her slight form, and a warm hood was upon her head.

"Edith, with her lovely dark-blue pelisse trimmed with fur, her beautiful swan down tippet and cuffs, and her chinchiller hat trimmed with rich ribbon, and tied under her sweet little chin with the same, her curls showering all around beneath her jaunty little hat upon her tippet and coat. She looked very lovely, and so her mother thought, as she drew the bright creature close beside her, and motioned the little Nora to take the back seat. Nora gazed at her as if she had never before seen such a vision, and she thought to herself, 'Why am I so miserable and so poor, and *she* — ? but no matter, I love her, she is good to me.'

"Mrs. Vandyke loaded the carriage with all kinds of things, then making Nora give the direction to the driver they set off.

"O, what a hole of wretchedness was that!

so dirty, so dark, and damp; the child ran in exclaiming, 'O mother, I have not sold any matches, but see! O see! what good angels have brought us.'

"The room was so dark that she did not perceive, for an instant, (coming in so from the light of snow and sun,) that her mother lay upon the floor apparently struggling in the agonies of death. There was no fire, and the two children were closely wrapped up in an old dirty comforter, hugging each other tightly, and gazing with a terrified, bewildered look at their mother.

"Nora flew to her side, took her hand, then wiped the cold damp from her brow, and begged her to speak once more.

"She heeded nothing save her poor, dying mother; the little girl, the kind lady, all, all were forgotten then; little Edith clung trembling and horrified to her mother, and looked up imploringly to be taken away.

"And her mother took her back into the carriage, feeling it was too great suffering, too much of a shock, for one so young, and so unused to anything but joy.

"Then she returned and helped the frightened Nora to attend upon her dying parent.

"She spread some blankets she had brought over the heap of rags in one corner, and together they moved the poor woman into the bed, and covered her warmly with shawls, and after administering a warm drink with wine, the woman was more quiet, and soon her lips moved as if trying to speak. Nora eagerly bent down her head in order not to lose a word.

"'Have you come back, my poor, poor child? I thought you were frozen, and the terror that thought has given me, — Ah, my last hours have been such an eternity of suffering, all caused by my own sins!'

"'I am dying,' she gasped; 'I have been so cruel, so wicked; but want, starvation, has caused--all—and—then, I drank—to drown my miseries,—and became a fiend! Nora, —child,—come nearer. Let me kiss you,— forgive me,—pray for me, God will hear you, —you are so good. Let me see—Jessie— Alice,—one kiss,—and now I go; God bless

— *lady*, see to my little ones, — O God ! O God! forgive me !—I cannot see ; Nora open —O what a load ! Nora, bless—' She died with her sentence unfinished, and whatever her history ere she sunk so low was buried with her, — her language and her child's seemed to betoken better days.

"Nora clung around the wretched, squalid body, in an agony of grief, — for as bad as her mother had been to her, *she* was the only one in the wide, wide world who had ever cared for her, except her sisters ; her father had left them to their fate, long ago, after abusing their mother and them in all ways (so Nora told the lady afterwards) ; she felt desolate, altogether desolate, and her sobs were piteous ; the little ones cried, too, because sister did, for they had been so in the habit of seeing their mother lie for hours and hours, perfectly inanimate, that they realized nothing of the change.

"The kind lady, who had done so much, came gently up to them and said to Nora, 'My poor child, compose yourself, there is something to be done: now the best way for you to conquer yourself is to act; run into some of the neighbors and get them to come and get your mother ready for burial, — ask them, too, if you can get them to come at once, and say, also, there is a lady here who will pay them for all they do; then you must leave this room, you and the children; come with me; when all is ready for the burial you shall return to see your mother to her last resting-place.'

"Nora did as she was bid. By the light of the bright fire which the footman built, by Mrs. Vandyke's orders, the room and all its squalidness was displayed. 'Alas, alas, that human beings should ever be so degraded!' so thought Mrs. Vandyke; but did she know and realize all the miseries and horrible temptations of the poor, she would say, 'Alas, alas, that poverty should cause this degradation, and that so few there are to put out a hand to keep them from their misery!'

"Mrs. Vandyke took the poor, desolate orphans home after their mother's burial. The two little ones were placed in the Orphan Asylum; Nora she kept for her own maid, or rather for a companion to her little girl, — so little

Edith had a playmate, and one her mother never feared to trust her with; she proved herself lovable and useful, both mother and daughter were sorry in after years to part with her.

"A good, kind mechanic asked her for his wife, and one 'well to do in the world,' as Nora said. So Nora took both her young sisters to live with her, and a proud and happy day it was for her, when she welcomed them to her own pretty and pleasant home."

"O Belle, darling, don't that end nicely, and is n't it a pretty story? but now I am tired and must lie down, so help me to bed, won't you? and then don't leave me, for I so love to have you here."

Belle helped her to bed, tucked her in nicely, and then sat down beside her, with her book in her hand; she looked very thoughtful and sad; at last she exclaimed, "O Lilly! how I long to be a lady, that I may be able to go about and help these poor people, and make them happy, don't you?"

No answer; she looked towards her cousin, and found that she had sunk into a deep slumber.

Belle leaned over her for a few moments, thinking how beautiful she looked, although so pale and thin; her auburn ringlets were scattered over the pillow, one or two falling around and shading her face, and there was an expression of happiness and rest upon her features, that were seldom there when awake.

Lilly's sickness, however, had softened her very much, and the constant devotion of Belle endeared her to her heart, so that she obtained great influence; indeed, all the household loved sweet Belle, and Mrs. Mordaunt had not yet become so enervated by worldliness, that she could look without wonder and interest upon the gentle child, and she felt that there must be a light and a guide within her heart, which she herself had never known or acted by; this constant example, and the extreme peril that her idol had been through, opened her eyes to look within, to see what she had been living for, and to think how she had been neglecting the highest interests of that child she *thought* she loved so much. As her daughter gradually but surely changed, she looked upon life with a truer vision, and made resolutions, which were kept. Harry now came in for his share of devotion, and altogether they were a happier and a better family than before Lilly's sickness.

CHAPTER IV.

SCHOOL DAYS.

Lilly and Belle went to school together, as I believe I have mentioned before; but I have not spoken of their school, or their teachers, and, as Lilly will now soon be well enough to go once more, we will introduce you within its precincts.

It was a very large school, and an excellent one, too, although a free-school, and a great many rich and fashionable people sent their children there because it was so good.

Belle's father, Mr. Harley, knew all the plans and prospects, and was thoroughly convinced of the excellence of its systems; and it was principally that Belle might attend it, that she was sent to her aunt Mordaunt, and that aunt placing great confidence in the judgment of her brother, concluded to send Lilly and Harry there also.

The head teacher, Mr. Burbank, was a warm and dear friend of Mr. Harley; they were at college together, and had been like brothers to each other.

Mr. Burbank was no common-place person; he entered Cambridge under the most brilliant auspices. The only son of rich parents, his father high in position, and proud of that elevation acquired by himself; his most ambitious hopes, however, centered in this son, who was distinguished for his quick and brilliant talents, his remarkable personal beauty, and his generous, noble, and manly character; he graduated with the highest honors. Burbank and Harley, the inseparables, bore off the palm; and these noble, great-souled young men were also devoted Christians. About a year before they left college, their minds became interested and their hearts awakened; from mere philosophy and indifference they were aroused to a higher life, and they both resolved to devote themselves to the cause of truth and goodness. Harley became a minister of the gospel, and Burbank wished to spend his life in the cause of education. For several years he was spending time and money in travelling over the United States, visiting schools, establishing them where there were none; and then, to complete his parent's chagrin, he turned teacher himself, and now for the last five years he had been Principal in this large free-school, with eight or ten teachers under him. What wonder that Mr. Harley wished to send his treasure to such a man to learn the ways of wisdom!

This is a long digression from my heroines, but I trust my young readers will not find it uninteresting, and they will better understand the influences which were surrounding and guiding our young friends, for most particularly did this good man watch over and interest himself in the little ones of his flock. He had never married, but yet his heart was full of love and gentleness to children, and his friend's child was like a sunbeam in his path; he longed, whenever he saw her, to take her in his arms and tell her how dear she was to him, but he refrained, and never in school hours did he allow any partiality to her to influence him in the least.

The good in the school loved and revered their teacher, and glad and proud were they when a word of praise or a smile of approbation rewarded them for a well-learned lesson or a praiseworthy action.

The bad and mean and envious in the school (for, alas! there were such) were afraid of him, and glad to keep out of the reach of that searching eye.

Among the children that surrounded him, the two he loved most were Belle and Lilly, but he felt more compassion, more earnest, yearning tenderness, for Alice Edmonds and her brother. He knew their desolateness, knew that no sweet and holy influences ever surrounded them at home, knew they needed most his care.

Alice had many noble qualities, but they were almost hid by a layer of pride and envy. Edgar was a beautiful, manly little fellow, but from constant indulgence had grown selfish, and, in consequence of little or no moral training, had acquired many bad and vicious habits.

But with him our story has little to do; his sister claims our attention, with the other girls.

It is the commencement of a new term. Belle and Lilly are both at school now, but were absent all the last part of the other term. It is February, and a very cold, snowy morning; the girls were welcomed back to school with great joy by nearly all the scholars, for Belle, in particular, was a great favorite.

A knot of girls are assembled around her desk now, it being intermission; among them, Julia Talbot and Alice Edmonds.

"O Belle," said Julia, "do you like our new teacher, Miss Manners? I thought you would feel so badly when you came back to find our dear Miss Millar gone, she was so pretty and so sweet; but do you like this one, Belle?"

"I don't know yet, Julia; she seems to be sad and reserved, and not so much interested in us as Miss Millar, but perhaps she will like us better, by and by."

"Well, for my part," said Alice, "I can't bear her, with her proud, stuck-up ways. I don't believe I shall ever like her, although she reads and draws so beautifully."

"But, Alice, don't you remember how good she was one day to that poor child, Jenny Gray, when she fell down and tore her dress, and hurt herself so badly. You know the child felt worse about the dress than anything else, for she said her mother would be so angry; so Miss Manners spent the whole intermission in mending it for her so neatly you would hardly have known it had been torn."

"I dare say you will like her, Julia, for she favors you particularly, I don't know why, — she did n't let you go down the other day until you had two chances, and then she seemed sorry; for my part, I have nobody to favor me. 'I care for nobody — nobody cares for me;'" and singing that, she walked away. An expression of pain, however, was upon her features, and she evidently hummed the air to keep down the rising tears. Julia saw the expression and hastened after her, and putting her arm around her waist they went out of the door together.

Belle left her desk and ran out to exercise

in the open air a few minutes. She met at the door several of the school girls.

"O, how cold, how bitter cold it is! You had better stay in the house, Belle." But Belle was off in a moment.

"Why can't we always have summer, it is so much pleasanter; I hate winter."

"O, I don't, Letty! I love winter, the snow is so beautiful, and the icicles that hang glittering in the sun, sparkling like diamonds, and the frost work on the window-panes, I do so love to see all these, and then the air makes my cheeks glow, and I feel so bright and so joyous I wish it was winter always."

"And not so much wonder you do love it, Bessie, for you live in a great big house that's always warm; you ride to school very often, and you are all wrapped up in furs; and you have plenty of people to wait upon you, so that you never need go in the cold only when you like. But I have to wait on myself, and help others, and to go into cold rooms and work until my fingers are stiff, so when play time comes I am quite willing to stay by the fire and keep warm."

"Why, Letty, I did n't know you had anything to do, you are always punctual at school and generally know your lessons; when do you learn them, if you have so much to do?"

"Evenings, to be sure; and that is the pleasant part of winter, to sit by the nice blazing fire, and have a bright light and the round table; then I feel as if I loved it. But, Bessie, did you see that woman and little child sitting on the church steps as we came to school? poor things, I guess they did not think the snow beautiful, or the icicles either!"

"For poor folks," said Bessie, thoughtfully, "it is bad, — I did n't think of them. No! I did not see the woman; tell me about her."

"I did n't stop, for I thought I was late to school, besides I had nothing to give, and it was of no use. I wonder the bell don't ring; what a long intermission we are having!"

At this instant, in flies Lilly Mordaunt, her hood half off her head, her curls flying in every direction, her cheeks flushed, and her eyes sparkling with excitement.

"O, girls, girls! come out quick and see this woman in the yard, and this beautiful child. Miss Manners is talking to the woman in some foreign language, and she seems to know her, and was very much surprised to see her; do come girls, you never saw such a sorrowful-looking little girl, although so pretty."

"Where did you come across them, Lilly?" said Letty, as they both followed her out. "I guess it is the same couple I was just speaking of to Bessie."

"I found them in the street, and the child was so cold I took hold of her hand to make her come in, and the lady followed; but seeing so many in the yard the child was frightened, and ran clinging to her mother, and I could not get them in the house; so I went and called Miss Manners, and was n't it queer that they knew each other?"

It was some time ere the teacher returned; when she did, she explained to the scholars. The poor forsaken creature they saw was once at boarding school with her, — a French girl, sent and supported by wealthy parents, but she ran away from school with an Italian adventurer, who called himself Count. Her friends had in consequence cast her off, her husband proved worthless and had since died, and now she was alone in the world, with this child to support,—for she scorned to call upon the relatives who had so coldly deserted her. "I have taken her to my home. My girls, I see you are all interested in her and that lovely child; let us all try what we can do for them. But no more at present; to your desks, to your lessons."

Without a word the girls glided to their desks, but their hearts were full of the poor strangers.

As for Lilly, her lessons were half learned, the sad, dark eyes of the little Italian girl were floating all the time on the page before her, and when asked where the Pilgrim Fathers first landed, she answered, "In France!" much to the amusement of the whole class; even Miss Manners smiled, although she had to check the mirth, and gently reproved Lilly for her badly-learned lesson.

After school the girls, with their teacher, who really seemed to have thrown off her usual reserve, formed a plan for the relief of the sufferers: a contribution was to be taken from all the girls in their room; for the two to board, at present; and after Madame D'Osina's powers had been tested as a French teacher, she would be provided with a situation in the school, as they were in need of a good instructor in that department; little Maddalena was to be a scholar. *All* were interested in the project, even Alice Edmonds; and Miss Manners smiled so pleasantly upon them as they grouped around so eagerly, that some of them wondered how she could ever have seemed cold and stern to them.

We cannot hear the talk of all our young friends, so we will follow our favorites, Belle and Lilly, and listen to their earnest colloquy.

"Belle, what shall I do? I am afraid I can't give anything, — all my pocket money has gone. O, how sorry I am that I bought that set of China! it cost a dollar and a half, and I might have had all that for the sweet little girl, and now I have not a cent; what will you give, Belle?"

"I have but a dollar, Lilly, and that I intended to buy the Arabian Nights with, I do want it so much; but I must wait a little longer yet before I get it."

"Why, Belle, what did you do with those two dollars that your father sent you a month ago for pocket money?"

Belle blushed deeply, and said, "O! it is all gone, dear Lilly. I bought me a drawing-book and pictures, you know, and pencils."

"Yes, yes, but those did not cost more than a dollar; come, Belle, tell what have you been buying that no one has seen?"

"O, I have a dollar left!"

"Yes, but you had a dollar when those two came, so you must have spent it some way."

Thus pushed, Belle was obliged to own the truth.

"Lilly," she replied, "don't you remember the poor image boy that fell and broke his whole board full of figures that day in the street, when it was so slippery? You know how distressed he was, and how sad he looked. I whispered to him to come to me the next day, and I would help him a little towards replacing them. I gave him that extra dollar, and if you could have seen how grateful he was, you would be as glad as I that I had it to give, it did me so much good."

"Belle, what a queer girl you are! why did n't you want to tell me? You are always giving away your money, I do believe, for you have very few toys and you never buy candy, and yet you are just as happy, and happier, than I am, and I am always spending my money in candy and toys. I do wish I could be like you. O dear! what shall I do now for some money? I must ask mother to give me some more."

"But then, Lilly, it won't be your gift; you won't be doing anything for them, it will be your mother's."

"That's true; I wish I could, but it's no use wishing, and the money will do just the same good."

"Well, Lilly, if *you* really want to help *yourself*, I'll tell you what to do. You know your mother intended to get you a new silk apron like Alice's; why can't you tell her you would rather have the money, and then you can give a dollar to them, and have another left for the image boy and his poor little sisters?"

Lilly looked rather downcast; she could not

bear to give up the beautiful silk apron, and yet she longed to help, — the sacrifice was a *very great* one to her, for the love of dress was already one of her " besetting sins."

" O Belle," at last she exclaimed, " how can I give up that, when I have been wishing for it so long! I told Alice only to-day that mine would be prettier than hers. No, no, Belle! that is too much, I can't do that; but I will save my next pocket-mor , and pay mother what I borrow."

" But, Lilly, it is six weeks before you have your next allowance, and you know aunty said when you had the last that you must make it do you, for you could not have any more until it was time."

" I will teaze her, Belle, and I know she will give up just this once."

" O Lilly, darling! if I could only persuade you to try the other way now, and just see if you won't be happier than the silk apron could make you; and then we will each go to school to-morrow with our dollars, and feel that *we* have made them happier, — that *we* ourselves have done good."

"Here we are home already! I declare, I scarcely felt the cold, did you, Lilly? and yet see the icicles hanging from the roof, and see the trees in the garden, how beautifully the branches glisten in the sun, all encased as they are in the ice! it must be very cold."

"Yes! it is *so* cold my fingers are almost frozen; but, Belle, dear, about the apron." And she looked very serious.

"We will talk about it again, and in the mean time think it over, Lilly."

"O Lilly! O Belle! come — come into the yard, do!" and Harry ran to them all out of breath, and clapping his hands to keep warm. "I want you to see the great snow man I have been making; I made it all myself, and it is splendid!"

"No, no, Harry! I can't," said Lilly; "I am too cold, I must go in and warm myself."

"Well, Belle, now you will come, won't you? Lilly never does care about my fun."

"O yes, she does, Harry, but you know Lilly is n't very strong, and she is cold now; but I am not, and I would love to see your snow man, — how I do love to be out in this cold, clear, bright air! O, if I were a *little* girl again, and could slide down hill in your sled!"

"And what are you but a girl, Belle? and why should n't you slide down hill? Come along, do, and I'll fix you all nicely, and we will have such sport. There is a nice hill close by, so we will look at the man and then go there."

"No, no, Harry! indeed I am too old and too large for such play now, aunty says, and I must not disobey."

"Well, any way, I can draw you around the yard in my cutter, and then we can build a fort and snowball it, and have a fine time. I am so glad you love to be out, I never thought you would be such a good hand to play, you are so little, and so thin and white."

"Why, Harry, how you compliment! I thought I was getting very fat and large ever since I came, I have grown so much, and uncle says I am really rosy. So you need n't tell me I am like a ghost any more."

"O no, Belle! I did n't mean you looked bad; O, no indeed! but so different from Lilly, with her fat, round face. But I love to look at you better, you look so pleasant always."

The snow man was admired, and after a fine play in the yard, which gave them great appetites, they went in together to dinner.

And Lilly! where was she all the time? She was sitting in the library with her feet upon the fender before a bright wood fire, and looking intently into it, deeply meditating.

Her mother was there too, and she watched with something of a mother's pride the thoughtful, lovely face of her little Lilly. After a while she broke the stillness: "My child, what are you thinking about that keeps that busy tongue of yours still so long?"

"Wait a little, mamma dear, and I will tell you all about it; but first I want to make up my mind."

So she was still a few minutes longer, then jumping up she threw her arms around her mother's neck, and exclaimed, "Yes, I will do it, I will, — I won't have the apron, and I will have the money!"

"What is the matter with you? and what is all this about the apron and the money? you crazy little girl, you!"

"O mamma, little Lena and the French woman! I want the money for them, for dear, sweet little Lena."

"Try and compose yourself, my child, and tell me all you mean. I don't understand you, at all."

"Well, I will; now listen, mamma, and then give me what I want."

So Lilly told quite a connected story about the strangers, which we will omit, as you know it already.

"And now, mother, I want you to give me the money that silk apron would cost which you promised me, and let me give it to them, that is all."

The tears came into Mrs. Mordaunt's eyes at this new proof of Lilly's efforts to conquer herself, and she thought, "O, that I may learn of these children lessons of life and of wisdom which can never leave me!"

The money was readily given, and the next day the two girls, as happy as queens, placed their dollars into the teacher's hand;— their faces were radiant with goodness and love.

Alice Edmonds's feelings were greatly

touched also by this tale of distress, and she brought all her savings for some time and handed them in, saying, she had rather spend it so than in the story books she meant to have bought.

Miss Manners gave her a sweet, approving smile, as she handed her contribution, and Alice was rewarded even then. "O may be," she thought, "I can make her love me, and so few do! O, why is it I cannot be more winning, like Belle Harley? or more beautiful, like Lilly Mordaunt? I do believe I am beginning to love Belle a little, after all." Alice's head was full of these thoughts as she went back to her desk. Belle noticed her sad expression again, and thought, "I wish Alice liked me better, and would ever seem glad to see me. I don't think she is very happy, and I would love her if she would let me, but she is so unkind to me; well, I suppose I must love her in spite of it; by and by, she will understand me better." How little did Belle know, at that very instant, that Alice's heart was warming towards her! Thus it is in this world, we know not the hearts of those around us; let us be careful then, even in our lightest words or actions, to spare the feelings of all.

But in our digression we have left our school to take care of itself.

Mr. Burbank came in, in the course of the morning, to say that there would be a public examination at the end of the next quarter, five months from that, nearly. There would be four prizes awarded to that room: the first for the most disinterested and best behavior in all respects, the next for the best scholarship, the third for the finest composition, and the fourth for the best drawing. The prizes were, first, a small rosewood cabinet, inlaid with pearl, in which were twelve volumes of the best works for children; the second, a very elegant papier-mache writing desk; the third, a gold pen and pencil; the fourth, a valuable and very handsome paint-box.

"I tell you thus early," Mr. Burbank went on to say, "in order that all may have a fair and long trial. Some have been sick this quarter, and some have been absent. Now girls, all exert yourselves, and let us see at the next public examination what pride and glory we shall have in you. At the end of this quarter there will be our usual examination; all the marks will be preserved in order to show the progress as we advance." He talked to them all in a kind, affectionate manner some time longer, asked a good many questions, which were answered very promptly by many voices, and then left the room.

The girls' eyes shone with delight, and each little heart resolved to win the victory.

Alice Edmonds was now the head of all in her studies. Her mind was uncommonly bright and active, but she was often lazy, and sometimes stayed at home from choice, and sometimes from sickness; so that Belle, who came next, and Julia Talbot next, often stood higher. Of this quarter, about six weeks had passed, and Belle had been absent half of it, owing to Lilly's sickness. Now, however, she was determined to make up for lost time; she longed to win the prize in scholarship to please her dear father, whom Belle loved with a devotion few children display towards their parents. Since her mother's death her heart was more closely than ever entwined about her father, and to please him was *one* of the greatest objects of her life. The separation was a bitter trial for both, but harder for the father; his one ray of sunshine, his loving comforter, his sweet daughter, to part from her was sad indeed, but for her sake he could do it, and his sacrifice will be rewarded; there was no good school where he lived and was settled, and his own duties were too onerous to attend, as he wished, the education of Belle. Other motives, too, impelled him to send her to his sister. Mrs. Mordaunt was the only sister, — he had always loved her with the most tender love; she was still very young, only twenty-five, and very beautiful. He knew her heart had been untouched by the spirit which alone could give true joy and peace, knew she was gay and worldly, and he wisely thought the constant presence of his lovely and pure child, the influence of her simple, natural, and fervent piety, would be an unfailing and daily example which would be hard to resist. "Out of the mouths of babes and sucklings has Thou ordained praise." His heart yearned, too, over the beautiful little

Lilly; he knew his sweet flower would impart some of her own fragrance to the most neglected garden, so he let her go, feeling he had done wisely. Her little brother was but two years old, and of course but little comfort to him; and as he was sickly he was very backward. They both seemed to inherit their mother's frailness of constitution, and the father trembled as he gazed upon their transparent complexions and large, brilliant eyes.

But to return to our scholars after this long digression. We left them quite excited by the prospect of being victors. A few moments after Mr. Burbank left the room, intermission was given; the girls separated into cliques, and were eagerly discussing the subject of the prizes.

"I suppose," said Alice Edmonds, "Belle Harley takes it for granted she will get the prize for goodness; but she won't for anything else, at any rate."

The tears came to Belle's eyes at this unkind remark, and she turned away her face, without speaking.

"For shame! Alice Edmonds, — for shame!

why do you take such pains to be ugly to Belle Harley? I am sure she is always good to you."

"It is nothing to you, Bessie Gray, what I say to any one. I think she has a tongue, and can speak for herself."

"Yes," said Belle, recovering herself, "I can speak; but I am afraid I have nothing to say you will wish to hear, for all I can say or do will not change your feelings towards me, and I think perhaps I had better be silent."

"O Belle," said Lilly, "you are too meek by half! Why don't you give Alice as good as she sends? I would, I guess."

"Well, I wish she would. I do believe I should like her better if I could make her angry; but no matter what I say, she is always just so patient and looks like an injured martyr, and it provokes me; why should she be so different from the rest of us?"

"I know," said Lilly, in reply, "that *I* love her better than I do all the rest put together; and I know, too, that when I am the best I love her the most, and if you were more amiable may be you would, too."

"Well, Lilly Mordaunt, I don't think *you* will make me more amiable. I sha'n't come to you, *little miss,* for lessons."

"No one wants you to," replied Lilly, still more warmly; "the less you come to me the better."

"O hush, hush, Lilly! don't talk so, and get so angry. Indeed, you will only make Alice dislike me more; besides, you are unkind now."

"I don't care! her love is n't worth having, and she sha'n't abuse you to me." And the warm-hearted child threw her arms around Belle's neck.

Belle kissed her affectionately, and turning to Alice, said, "Don't be angry with Lilly, Alice, for it was in her love for me she forgot herself."

"O," said Alice, turning away and walking off, "I don't care what she says; it makes little difference to me. As I say often, 'I care for nobody, nobody cares for me.'"

Julia, Lettie, and Bessie, and the sweet little Lena (Lilly's sworn friend), too, cast indignant glances at Alice as she left them, and the words *ugly, mean, shameful,* were muttered; and she caught them all, as she strode off alone.

Poor girl, how much more is she to be pitied than the one she sought to annoy! and at this moment, if her pride would have allowed, she would have asked Belle's pardon for her unkindness; it was envy that made Alice so unjust. Before Belle came to the school, she was first, not in the girls' affections, but as leader and ruler, and she could not bear a rival; so all her bad qualities were brought out, which, as long as she could rule, did not appear. She was generous, bright, and full of fun and frolic, and with a strong will she had in a measure led all the girls. They referred to her in all cases of dispute, as well as amusement, and often had her imperious temper made the quarrel, which might have been healed by a peacemaker, more vehement and the parties more bitter against each other.

Since Belle came among them, gradually all this changed. Belle was the arbiter, Belle was the judge; the little girls seemed to feel that her rule was the best; her sweet, soothing spirit and her gentle words of counsel, with the help of her motto, "Do unto others," &c., always had their effect. The golden rule came to be a motto for others, as well as herself, and almost all the *little* girls wrote it in all their books. This state of things vexed and irritated the proud spirit of Alice, and made her act at times as if she hated Belle.

The conversation continued after Alice's departure. Julia Talbot remarked that she thought little Jennie Gray would get the prize for conduct, for she is never naughty, and never does wrong in school.

"I think so too, Julia," answered Belle, "and I do hope so, for the dear little thing will be so delighted."

"Why, Belle, don't you want it? I am sure she is not better than you are," said Lilly.

"Yes she is, Lilly dear, and she has improved far more than I have; with naturally a quick temper, she tries harder than I do to conquer it, and then too she is more careful. I am often reproved for leaving my books about, and she never; now carelessness is bad conduct, or leads to wrong, always."

Bessie. "Yes, you have that fault, and that is the only one I know, Belle, and *you* think more of that than any one else does. If I could only be as good as you are, how happy I should be, and how happy I could make mother!"

Belle. "Bessie, it makes me sad to have you talk so; how little you know me! O, how much I do and say and feel every day and hour that is wrong, and yet I do not mean to disparage myself; I know I try very hard, and that is a good deal. But, Bessie, do not take me for a pattern; take Him, who was once a little child, and who blessed little children; He, who gave us our rule, that beautiful rule which we have all written in our books now, and I trust in our hearts, too."

"What is it?" said little Lena; "tell *me*, won't you? I never heard any rule, except *ma mère* tells me never to trouble any one, or to be rude, and always to obey."

"Lilly will tell you, darling, she has practised it so well in regard to you."

"O hush, hush, Belle! pray don't tell her that!"

"Yes yes, do tell me! what did Lilly do for me, that I don't know? she is always helping me in some way, — dear Lilly;" and Lena ran and threw her arms around her affectionately.

"Well, well, Lena! come away with me and I will tell you all about Belle's 'golden rule,' as she calls it."

"Not *mine*, Lilly! although *I* would like to follow it."

Lena and Lilly went off, hand in hand.

Lena was already the pet and plaything of all the girls; she was only five years old, and very small for her age, and thoughtful as most children of twelve, — made premature by want and suffering. Her large, lustrous eyes were intensely sad in their expression, her clear dark complexion unrelieved by a shade of pink, her mouth and teeth beautiful, and her hair fell in soft waving curls of jetty black nearly to her waist; should she get fat and rosy now that she is so happy, dimples might play about that cherub mouth, and some of the spirituality of expression might give place to a more child-like and gleesome look.

Lilly having been the first one to notice the child and make her known, the first one who had brought joy to her heart, she attached herself with peculiar fidelity to *her;* to be *near her,* to run for her, to do any little service in any way, was joy enough for Lena.

Julia, Bessie, Lettie, and Belle, talked for some time longer about the examination, and when the bell rang they were in the midst of a discussion about a picture. Belle and Julia had to copy a landscape of great beauty; Julia thought it too difficult, but Belle liked it because there was so much foliage; Julia liked best to draw water scenes, so she determined to ask Miss Manners to allow her to change it for William Tell's chapel,—which request was afterwards complied with.

CHAPTER V.

THE LAST DAY OF THE QUARTER.

The months sped quickly by, although to some of those anxious hearts they seemed to drag along. The girls had all done marvellously well the last quarter, so Miss Manners encouragingly told them, and to some of them her beaming looks of love and approbation were of more value than even the prizes; well had they all learned to love that reserved teacher, as they used to call her,—to win her smiles, and to receive an affectionate word, was as much striven for as good marks; even Alice loved her, and tried more than ever she had done in her life before to obtain her love,—how well she succeeded, time must prove.

And now the last day of the quarter had arrived.

Lilly came home from school the day before, in a great state of excitement.

"Mother! mother!" she cried, as soon as inside the doors, "where are you?" and she flew to the library; "mother, to-morrow is the day, — the examination, — and you and father must come! and Belle and I must wear our nicest dresses, for there will be ever so many people there; and O, mother, you don't know how few bad marks I have had this quarter, and how high I stand in my studies! I don't —"

"Well, well, Lilly, child; stop a moment now to take breath! Have you run all the way from school, that your hair is all flying in every direction, your bonnet half off and cheeks so very red? do you expect to get a prize, that you are so excited, dear?"

"O no, mother, I don't! only perhaps a medal or a token from Miss Manners, to show I have improved; for, mother, how could you suppose that *I* could stand higher than Belle, or Julia, or Alice, or ever so many others older and smarter?"

"But I think there should be prizes awarded

to the smaller children, or if not, then the prizes should be given to those who have improved the most, in comparing the last quarter with this; not to the *one* or *ones* who have the most marks."

Belle, who had come in during this last observation, replied: —

"And so it is to be, aunty, — that is the way I understand Mr. Burbank; and Lilly will have one, I rather think, for I heard Miss Manners say to Mr. Burbank, she thought Lilly Mordaunt had *improved* more during the last four months than *any* girl in school; there was a great change in her."

"Did you, Belle, did you? O, how glad I am! for now I can feel as if I could in time be of some use to dear little Lena. It is all you, Belle; I never thought of trying to be good until you came here."

The tears came to Mrs. Mordaunt's eyes; Lilly saw them in a moment and sprang to kiss them away, — "O mother, dear, I did not mean to — to — "

"I know, Lilly, my darling, you did not mean to reproach your mother; it was involuntary, but deserved, dear. Yes, my Lilly, I feel that I owe as much as you to our dear Belle. God was good when he sent her among us."

"It is God who has come to your heart, it is all his spirit, — I am only a little child of his sent to love you all; but I am so happy, so very happy, when I can think that I have been of use to those I love so dearly."

"How happy we all are together, mother dear! Harry and I now can agree very well, and it seems to me I love *everybody* a great deal better than I used to."

"That is always the way, dear child; when we forget ourselves in others, we not only make them, but us, gainers. I have learned a great deal in the last year, as well as you, Lilly, and feel as if I had only now begun to live; when I felt as if God was taking away from me my treasure, then my eyes began to open. Ah, my Lilly, may *you* never suffer as I have!"

Lilly was seated in her mother's lap; she threw her arms around her neck, and looked up at her with earnest love in her sweet eyes;

her mother kissed her tenderly and left the room.

It would be impossible to give an account of each and every day of those four months, so we have taken the liberty of passing over time, and bringing you to the very morning of the examination. All school-girls know what school-life is,—its joys and sorrows, its excitements,—and therefore we only wish to seize the principal events, and endeavor in *those* to show our little friends and their companions so that they may be to you living characters, and that you, my little readers, may make them your friends.

We must say a word of Alice, who has during the whole of the last quarter kept very much to herself, and studied diligently; there is hardly a doubt but that she will get the prize for scholarship, as she has kept her place at the head of the class in spite of all efforts of others to dethrone her; even when sick she has studied, and never a day of absence;—her strongest motive and most powerful incentive being to keep the prize from Belle,—to conquer her. And now let us enter the room.

The girls have arranged it gracefully and beautifully, with wreaths of evergreen and paper flowers; the teacher's desk is a perfect bower, and flowers seem blooming in every direction, — above, below, around.

Miss Manners, the beloved teacher, has taken her place; her cheeks were tinged with a faint glow, and her eyes were moist with loving pleasure, as she looked around at the circle of girls, and then at the proof of their love for her.

A great many happy faces were assembled in the school-room that morning; most radiant of all was Lilly's. Belle's words had never been out of her thoughts; and a sweet, pleased expression made her face beautiful indeed.

Belle was a good deal excited also; she knew Alice and herself stood *even* now as to marks in lessons, and it all depended on to-day's recitations. The prize for drawing she felt almost secure about, for she had seen all the others, and she could not help thinking her own the best; besides, the drawing-teacher had often said that Belle Harley would get the prize, and upon this picture she had bestowed great praise.

Alice Edmonds looked pale and unhappy, although there was a triumphant sparkle in her eye that said plainly, I shall carry off some of the honors.

The girls were all neatly, and some very prettily, dressed; and many were the sweet faces that met your eye as you glanced around that sunny, pleasant school-room.

The visitors had arrived. And school girls know what a flutter the presence of visitors always causes in their hearts; there were forty or fifty ranged around the room.

The classes in arithmetic, grammar, geography, reading, and spelling all passed, and very finely, too; none missed, or *few* at least, on that day. Thus far Alice and Belle were alike, except that Alice stood at the head, which would give her the prize if she passed this day triumphantly.

Now came intermission. The girls all eagerly ran to their mammas, papas, uncles, or aunts; but Mr. Burbank enters, and smilingly welcoming the band of children, asked the visitors into his other apartments to listen to the boys awhile, as their intermissions were not at the same time. Then the children all rushed out, according to Miss Manners's advice, to have a play, and feel refreshed for the still harder duties coming, — all but Alice. She remained poring over her books, for she had had such a headache the night before that she could not study at all. There was no one in the school-room but Alice and Miss Manners, and Miss Manners was very busy at the desk, looking over and comparing marks.

Suddenly, Alice leaves her seat and goes to Belle's desk, evidently looking for something. She holds the desk open a long while. "How beautiful!" she utters; "O, she will get the prize for drawing, mine is nothing to it!" Well, it's only the third prize, she thought, let her have it.

A hasty movement of the arm caused an overthrow of something, then came an earnest and terrified ejaculation; she looks up and around, pale and frightened, but perceiving no one has noticed her, takes the book she was hunting for, looks into it for something, replaces it, and goes back to her own desk. All this time Miss Manners seemed wholly absorbed in her task, yet she had seen and heard all; not a word or a look betrayed that knowledge, for she wished to see what the result would be.

Miss Manners had long been watching Alice with interest, — had noticed her envy of Belle, knew her situation, her temptations, — knew, too, that she had many fine and noble qualities. She felt deeply interested in the girl, and wished to root out from her heart those unamiable traits which now not only made others, but herself, unhappy. She thought and *hoped* yet to see her two most brilliant scholars *friends*, *loving* friends, therefore she determined not to interfere in this matter, but to trust to Alice's nobler nature triumphing, and unless it were necessary for justice she would speak no word to implicate Alice.

Alice went back to her seat and tried to study; but, alas, she had lost the power! All her thoughts would fasten themselves upon the work of destruction she had accomplished, and although she did not really *intend* to do it, yet she was not *sorry* it was spoiled, and she was determined to keep *her secret*. No one will know who did it, and Belle, who is always rather careless, will think she knocked it over herself; she had no business to have left her cork out, she deserves it for that, and now I don't believe she will get any prize, and I'm glad of it. So she tried to think, and so she would say over and over to herself, and yet the vision of that lovely picture all defaced, and of poor Belle's sorrowful face when she saw it, would come between her eyes and the book, and make her uneasy and unhappy; in spite of herself, it was in vain to try to study.

Julia Talbot came up to her; she had just come in from a nice run.

"Come, Ally, do come out and exercise a little! you look as pale as if you had seen a ghost. I know you will feel better, and recite better, if you will."

"Well, Julia, I believe I will, for my head is throbbing so I can't study; besides, I know the lesson so well, the whole book pretty much I can repeat, I have studied so hard this winter."

So off they went. After a half-hour's play

the girls were all once more seated at their desks.

The history class was called; the girls came up before the teacher's desk and stood while reciting.

"Miss Edmonds, give a brief and clear account of the reasons our forefathers left their own shores, the manner in which they did so, also a portion of their subsequent history upon landing."

Alice began very well, looking bright and clear; but soon she hesitates, blunders, and mixes up her account in such a manner that Miss Manners, surprised, looked keenly at her, saying: —

"Collect yourself, Miss Alice, you are certainly thinking of something else; this is one of the simplest questions, one you surely can answer well if you will think one moment."

Thus rebuked, Alice recalled her wondering thoughts, commenced the answer again, and succeeded very well.

"You nearly lost your place this time," whispered Belle, "take care."

"Don't fear, you are not going to beat me this quarter, Miss Belle."

"Young ladies, no talking! Miss Harley, I am under the necessity of asking a question twice."

Belle blushed deeply, but feeling herself wrong, said nothing. However, she had lost one mark as well as Alice.

"Give an account of the Pequod war: its origin, progress, and termination."

The question was answered promptly and well.

Julia Talbot gave an account of the causes of the Revolution, and during it quite an amusing description of the overthrow of the tea, and some humorous anecdotes of the opposition to the stamp act.

Bessie Gray was called upon for a description of some of the principal battles, and the recital of the dangers and difficulties of our revolutionary veterans.

All acquitted themselves well upon this day at least, although some *far* better than others. Julia missed once, as also did Lettie Brown; but the class was an intelligent one, and they showed plainly they understood what they were studying.

I will not weary my young readers by a detailed account of each recitation, suffice it to say that they all passed off well, Alice still retaining her seat triumphantly until the class in mathematics was called. This was a hard trial for her, with her aching head and guilty thoughts; she was all mixed up in her ideas, got terribly confused, and at last answered wrong altogether; her problems were not demonstrated properly, and she made bad work of it; at last, pleading a severe headache, she left the class, and, mortified and ashamed, went to her seat.

In spite of all, she had failed, and Belle would glory over her. O, how she hated her just then, and how full her heart was of bitterness! Poor girl, she was indeed to be pitied.

What an expression of delight was upon Belle's sweet face when she found she had indeed obtained the victory; for although she felt sorry for Alice, it was not in a young girl's nature not to rejoice at the success for which she had worked so hard, and the flush of pleasure was upon her cheek as she passed to her seat; but she had to pass Alice, and then her joy vanished. Alice's face was buried in her hands, and she was sobbing bitterly.

Belle could not resist speaking, and leaning over, she whispered, "Alice, dear Alice, don't cry so; indeed, you deserve the prize after all, for it was only your sickness that caused your failure. I will say this to Miss Manners, and you shall not lose your place; so, dear Alice, cheer up."

Alice did not move, or speak. And then came a voice from the desk: —

"Miss Harley, out of order for the second time. I am surprised!"

Blushing all over her face, Belle went to her seat. Fortunately the lessons were all over, or I fear that Belle too would have missed.

Next the compositions were read, some of which were remarkably pretty, and would have done credit to older heads.

Julia Talbot's, upon school days, was beautiful. Bessie Gray's, upon poverty, had some fine thoughts, and was prettily expressed.

Belle's was upon poetry, and had in it a few verses of her own, which were very musical in their rhythm, although not strikingly original in thought. These over, Miss Manners called for the drawings.

There was a general opening of desks. Each young lady came forward in order to hand their picture, beginning with the one nearest the desk.

Alice was first, she came forward, but her usually pale face was crimson; this might have been the result of weeping. Next came Julia, and then Bessie Gray, and now was Belle's turn.

She moved not from her seat, but her head was bowed upon her desk, and she seemed weeping.

"Miss Belle," said Miss Manners, gently, "what is the matter? where is your picture, is it not finished? why those tears?"

Belle tried to speak but could not, at last Miss Manners stepped to her desk. Belle held up to her view the beautiful sketch, all defaced by streams of ink in every direction.

"How did this happen, Belle?"

"I don't know, indeed, but I suppose I must have left my inkstand open, and then overturned it without knowing it; but I looked at it just before I went out at intermission and it was all right, and I have not, that I remember, opened my desk since. O dear, I am so sorry! for this was to be a present,—a present to you, Miss Manners, and it was so pretty." And then her tears flowed afresh.

Alice,—how did she look and feel all this time? she tried to seem unconcerned, but her face had a guilty look, and if any one had suspected her they would have noticed it. Miss Manners gave her one glance, and knew *all* the story; but still she thought it best to wait a little longer, and let Alice's good feelings have time to come into her heart; she hoped yet for Alice.

So, speaking kindly to Belle, she said:—

"Never mind, my dear, don't distress yourself any more, we will examine into this matter; your picture still has enough left to show how beautiful it must have been, so look cheerful; Mr. Burbank will be in, in a few moments, to distribute the prizes."

Belle soon composed herself, and looked as bright as if nothing had happened. Mr. Burbank entered and the important business commenced.

"Young ladies," begun Mr. Burbank, "I find by the reports that Misses Belle Harley and Jennie Gray stand *highest* in their marks for conduct; but I also find that Miss Mordaunt, although she cannot number as many as *either* of them, has improved from last quarter more than any one in the school,— *in all respects*, her efforts have been great, and her success marked; in lessons, conduct, &c., she has conquered more than either of the others; to *her* then, with your consent, I shall give the first prize. Speak, Miss Belle, are you satisfied?"

"O yes, sir, indeed I am so very glad!" eagerly said Belle.

"Jennie, my little one, what do you say?"

"Yes sir, she deserves it," tremblingly said and softly; "but O, my mother will be so disappointed!" Jennie's mother was not there; she was too poor to leave her work.

"No, Jennie, she shall not be; I have the same or similar prizes for you and Belle also. I only wished to test your disinterestedness."

Jennie's little face now shone with delight.

"Step forward, young ladies, and take these gifts, and with them your teachers' love and approbation."

Next came the lesson prize.

"I find that Miss Belle Harley takes the laurels upon this occasion also; I thought it would have been a drawn game between her and Miss Edmonds, and therefore prepared two prizes. Miss Edmonds, however, has signally failed to-day. Miss Belle, come forward and receive the second prize."

Belle arose, but did not advance; with blushing modesty she said : —

"Mr. Burbank, the prize should be awarded to Alice; indeed, she has kept her place through the whole quarter, and often recited better than myself; she only failed to day in consequence of a severe headache, brought on too by close study. I cannot feel that I deserve to take the prize from her, sir. I should not be happy in doing so." And she seated herself again.

Mr. Burbank gave her a pleased, loving

glance, then turning to Alice, said, "Miss Edmonds, you are the next candidate; since Miss Harley refuses, we award the prize to yourself."

Alice stepped forward to take the prize, her face crimson and with no joyful look upon it; still she took it, curtsied, and went to her seat, while several of the girls whispered, "It is too bad!" Miss Manners gave her a look which made Alice wince; but not yet did she speak.

The composition prize was next awarded to Miss Talbot.

Then came the drawing prize. "Young ladies, Miss Harley's picture, which would have obtained the prize most likely, is spoiled, perhaps by her own carelessness; therefore the prize is Miss Edmonds's, who comes next."

Alice again arose, and was about to step forward, but a sudden emotion came over her; she stopped, burst into tears and said, "I don't deserve the prize, indeed I don't, not any prize, for I did it, I did it all, — for I am wicked and hateful. I never intended to tell any one; but Belle is so good, so generous, and I have been so unhappy; and now, if

Belle will only forgive me for my meanness it is all I ask." She seated herself, and buried her face in her hands Belle was very much moved, as also were all in school, and there was a long pause, for no one seemed able at once to speak; even the visitors were surprised into some emotion, for many of them knew Alice and her proud nature, — knew how much it had cost her to make so public a confession. Belle rose from her seat at length and looked towards Miss Manners, who seemed to divine her wish, and nodded in acquiescence. She went to Alice, put her arm around her neck, and whispered some loving words in her ear; then Alice looked up, and for the first time that morning, a happy, satisfied look rested upon her face. Belle returned again.

"Alice," said Miss Manners, gently, "I knew all this before. I watched you during intermission, saw you at Belle's desk, heard your exclamation of admiration, and then, soon after, your frightened ejaculation; and as soon as Belle's defaced picture was handed me the secret was told, but I was determined not to betray you unless it was absolutely necessary for justice. I saw you were unhappy, knew why you missed your lesson, and hoped and *believed* that your better nature would finally triumph. How closely I have studied you through the whole quarter, you will never know; but when I tell you I knew and *loved* your mother, that in my early childhood's days she was my best friend, then you will understand why I longed so much to have *you* noble and true and good, and to have you and Belle friends. The union which will now cement you two is worth more than all the rewards that gold or gems could procure; this *first* triumph over yourself is invaluable to you; now, I have but little fear that you will go on progressing."

Mr. Burbank now came forward. "Young ladies, I need not tell you how deeply gratified I am at this amicable ending of our quarter. I am sure that the love which you have fought for and obtained, dear Belle, is worth more to you than any prize I can bestow; and I am also sure, dear Alice, that you have been sufficiently punished for your faults towards Belle, whatever they were. Hereafter may you ever be warm friends. Strict justice, however, will not permit me to award the prize for studies to any but Belle, as it was your own misconduct and not sickness alone which caused your failure. The prize for drawing will not be awarded this quarter."

Miss Manners. "I have a token for Alice, which is my own gift, — a testimony of her triumph over herself, and of the warm love of her teacher." So saying, she handed Alice an elegant copy of the "Holy Bible."

After this many of the girls were presented with medals, one out of each class had some testimony of the approbation of their teachers.

Mr. Burbank. "And now, young ladies, you are dismissed. May we meet again in health and happiness, and may God bless you and be with you ever."

The examination was over, the important question of the prizes settled. There were many leave-takings after school; the good-by to Miss Manners was a most affectionate one. She certainly had succeeded in winning the love of all her scholars, and her eyes were moist with tears in parting from them; especially to Alice did she give a most warm embrace, trying to soothe her emotion and cheer her spirits; poor Alice wept bitterly as she clung with such affection to her kind teacher, and begged her to love her in spite of her faults.

Lilly and Belle went home full of joy and gladness; but Belle's greatest joy was that which her prize brought her not,— the glow which burned on her cheek and sparkled in her eye, the sweet smiles which played around her mouth, were caused by the consciousness that she had won another heart to love her, that she had been enabled "to overcome evil with good."

The excitement and the confinement proved too much for the delicate frame of Alice, and the next day she was unable to rise from her bed.

Belle went over there early in the morning, with messages from Mrs. Mordaunt and Lilly to bring her back to pass the day, but, alas! she was very sick; she stayed with her until night, tenderly watching over and attending to her slightest wish, and only left her when it was time to welcome her dear father, who arrived at six.

How often did Alice turn her weary, heavy eyes upon her friend, with a glance so full of gratitude and love that the tears filled Belle's at once! How beautiful it was to see the change in that proud, scornful nature! how beautiful to know and feel that *love* can conquer all things!

"Dear Belle," said Alice, softly, "how can you bear to be near me? how can you be so kind, so loving, to me? have n't I always tried to injure you, been even cross and unjust, and caused you so much grief and so many tears?"

"Don't talk about the past, Alice dear! you love me now, and I am more than satisfied; try and think of pleasant things now, Ally, and don't get sad, for it is bad for you."

"O Belle, if I could only live with you always! You don't know how little there is in my own home to make me happy or good; and now, too, father is going to bring home a new mother. I know I shall hate her, and then what will Edgar and I do? for even aunty will be gone, and she loves us, I know, dearly, although she don't seem to sometimes."

"Ally, dear, you must not talk so much, you are feverish and your head aches. Your aunt told me when she went out I must keep you very quiet; what will she say when she finds you are more excited, worse than ever? so keep quiet. I will not say now what I want to about your new mamma that is coming. When you get well we will talk, and I will ask father to get your aunt to let you go back with me home, and then perhaps you can go into the country with us all the first of July."

"O, that would be so nice, Belle! So you think we can be together all that time; it would be too good."

"Yes, I am most sure Nurse Randall could accommodate you and little Lena too, who is going with us, for she sleeps with Lilly, and you could sleep with me; but now, Alice, do lie down (for she had risen in her joy, and was quite flushed and excited) and keep quiet. I will read to you awhile, and may be you will sleep."

Belle opened Alice's beautiful Bible, and read a chapter or two from her favorite gospel, John's.

Alice lay very quietly for a long time, gazing at her sweet face, so full of purity and love, feeling within herself, "If I only had a spirit like hers, but it is of no use trying; her nature is different from mine, she was born so, I never could be as good."

Ah, Alice! that is a salve often laid upon the conscience to keep it quiet within us, but do we not know that although God has made us to differ, yet to each he has given strength and power to subdue their will, to fight against temptation, and to come off victorious; evil can always be resisted, sin always conquered; the greater the conflict, the more glorious the victory. "It is through struggles and temptations the bad become *good*, and the *good*, *angels*."

After awhile Alice fell asleep; then with a noiseless step Belle left her and went home, first sending in the girl to stay until Miss Edmonds returned.

CHAPTER VI.

THE OLD FARM AND ITS INMATES.

ALICE did not recover fast enough to go with Belle to her home, but she went with them all into the country. What a merry party it was! — Mrs. Mordaunt, Mr. Harley, Lilly, Lena, Belle, and Alice, and little Harry. How full their young hearts were with joy and glee, and how much pleasure they anticipated!

Maddalena's mother was still with Miss Manners; they became warm friends.

Mrs. D'Osina was young and very lovely, and, although headstrong and imprudent, was full of generous impulses and strong feelings. Her gratitude to Emily Manners knew no bounds, she could not bear to be away from her; and Miss Manners's clear judgment, and firm, steady principle, formed a good staff for

Adèle to lean upon, until by constant effort and prayer, and through trial and failure, she could infuse into her own nature a portion of the *strength* so needed.

The little Lena was constantly at Mrs. Mordaunt's. Lilly loved her dearly, and her mother delighted to have the children together. Lilly was three years older than Lena, and it was quite amusing to see the motherly, protecting air she assumed towards her. She, Lilly, was excessively pleased when she obtained consent for Lena to go with her to the country. "The dear child needs the free, fresh air badly enough," said her mother, "and I am glad to have friends so kind as to take her." So she went to Nurse Randall's.

Nurse Randall's was a very large old farm in a country village, about a day's ride on the railroad from Boston. Here it was that Mr. Mordaunt first saw the light, and Mrs. Randall was his nurse, for his mother died soon after his birth. She was quite old now, nearly seventy, but still retained her love for her foster-child, and his children were as dear to her, almost, as her own. She had a daughter married and living with her; this daughter had two children, a boy and girl, and *one* of her husband's children by a previous marriage; with the *last* we will linger awhile.

Poor little Essie Millar (everybody called her so, therefore we will)! and no wonder, for no one could look upon her shrunken and misshapen figure, with its long, apish arms, high shoulders, and short neck; no one could glance upon that deformed, sad, sullen-looking child, without feeling she was an object of commiseration.

A shudder almost involuntarily crept over you when she came near; you felt as if she might be an evil spirit in disguise.

But this miserable child had deep, intense passions, the strongest yearnings for love, and a most susceptible and sensitive spirit.

Until she was five years old (now she was twelve) she had *a mother*, an own mother, who loved her all the more deeply and tenderly for her terrible misfortunes.

Around that mother the poor child had clung until her frame was interwoven with hers. She loved her as children of five years old could never love, unless *they* like her had but the *one* being on earth to care for; unless *they, like her,* had been rendered precocious by suffering and deformity.

This mother was very frail and sickly, and Essie would watch over her as tenderly as the most experienced nurse; the little creature would give her medicine, would smooth her pillow and brush her hair, would listen to her faintest request, and never leave her bedside to play, and hardly to eat.

How often did that mother send up fervent prayers to the throne of grace for her poor, stricken child!

"Who, O who will care for the unfortunate one when I am gone? would that it might be His will to take us both together!"

When her mother was well, though, they had many bright days together; and every sorrow that her love could ward off was carefully kept from the little Essie.

She was taught to sew, and as young as she was she could read beautifully; then, too, she could sing, her voice was sweet beyond expression; even in speaking it involuntarily attracted your attention, so sad in its tone, and yet so rich in its liquid sweetness.

Sometimes when they were seated side by side, (for Mrs. Millar was seldom strong enough to hold her,) Essie's tiny hand clasped in her mother's, and her large, sorrowful eyes fixed upon her, their sweet voices would mingle together until one who listened, unseen, might imagine angels were chanting some low, sweet hymn. Ah! those were halcyon days for poor Essie, and never did the child forget; their memory ever kept a pure place in her heart.

Their house was two miles distant from the nearest neighbors, so she had only her darling mother and good old Jemmy near her.

Mr. Millar was out at work all day, only coming in at his meals; and he seldom noticed the poor, deformed child, although she eagerly ran to attend his slightest want or call; he never gave her a glance of affection or a loving word. If he chanced to look at her at all, he would turn away his eyes again quickly, as if the sight pained him. Essie, however, would have her mother's smile of approval whenever she did anything for him, and that was reward enough.

The tears would spring to her eyes sometimes if her father spoke harshly to her mother, or "wondered" why she made such a fuss over that child.

"Why is it," she said one day, "why is it father hates me so, mother? is it because I am so ugly, so different from the little cousins he brought here one day to play with me? How he petted Nellie and kissed Bessie, and never a word or look for poor little me! I felt then as if I almost hated *them*, but *that went away*; but, O mother, if I were only beautiful like you!"

"Hush, hush, my child! you must not murmur at the burden God has given you to bear. If you are not beautiful, my daughter, you have a kind heart and a loving spirit, a mind quick to learn anything you wish, and a sweet voice to sing God's praise. Surely, if your form is crooked you have no right to complain, my love!"

"But, mother, father never asks to hear me sing, — never wants to see me."

"Your father does not know his child yet, my little Essie; perhaps one of these days you may be his greatest comfort." (Essie's eyes sparkled at this.) " He is absorbed in getting rich now, and he is disappointed, too, that his only child should be sickly and — "

"Deformed! yes, say it, mother; you need not be afraid to tell me so now, Nellie and Bessie said I was hideous, and had a hump and a dwarf's face." And she broke into a wild burst of tears. Her mother soothed her gently with words of love, and smoothing back her beautiful brown curls that fell around her in showers, said softly, —

"My Essie, do you wish to make your mother unhappy and sad? do you wish to grieve her so much, that she cannot sleep peacefully and quietly?"

O, how quickly were those arms, which the girls had jeered at, but one being *loved*, thrown around that mother's neck, and the broken words came forth, —

"Forgive me, mother, dear, darling mother! I will *never* complain again, — never, while I have you to love me."

Poor child, not six weeks after this that gentle mother lay cold in death, and Essie almost as cold and quite as inanimate beside her. No motion, no sign, seemed to show life, unless some one tried to take her from the body; then she would struggle and scream like a maniac, and it was dangerous to her to attempt it.

At last, she was worn out, and fell back entirely senseless; then she was removed. When her senses returned, she saw a strange face bending over her, a strange, hard face; this was her aunt, her father's sister, a maiden-lady, and quite rich; here she lived, until about a year before she was introduced to you at Nurse Randall's. Every year found her more and more sullen and morose, more wrapped up in an impenetrable sort of gloom and reserve.

Miss Millar did not mean to be unkind to the "*poor, deformed thing*," as she always called her, and yet she had no tenderness in her heart, and knew not how to call forth the good and sweet there was in the sad child; she never had the least powers of judging character; to her, Essie appeared not only ugly-looking but cold, ungrateful, and sullen.

She could not understand the workings of that poor suffering heart; she did not know that the silence which glued her tongue, whenever her aunt would speak of her departed mother, was a silence which was almost breaking her heart; and yet to *her*, to that cold woman, Essie could not talk of her who was enshrined in the innermost recesses of her soul; her grief, too, was grief which could not be spoken, — so Miss Millar thought she had soon forgotten her mother, " never spoke of her, and never shed a tear," and although every day her cheek grew paler and her shrunken form still more emaciated, yet it was all unnoticed, by one not accustomed to watch her. Before a month passed away, however, she was raving in the delirium of a brain fever. O, in her conscious intervals, how fervently did she pray for her death, how piteously in her ravings did she call upon her dead mother to come and take her poor, forlorn, desolate Essie to live with her!

Then, her obtuse aunt found out something of the depth of affection and the intensity of sorrow there was in that poor little heart.

She determined to be more kind to her, and she really nursed her with great devotion; she recovered, and was as well again as usual, but her frame was very delicate, always liable to severe sickness. Essie was not grateful for her recovery, on the contrary she wished her aunt had let her alone, so that she might have died and gone to her mother. This Miss Millar thought very ungrateful after all her nursing, but she did not say so, for really pity for the child had made her quite careful of her feelings. But alas, for Essie! she arose from her sickness more shut up within herself than ever; she would go whole days without speaking one word, and after a good many ineffectual attempts to win her confidence, Miss Millar let her alone, thinking the fever had deranged her mind, and that she was half idiot. All she needed bodily she had, but, alas! there was no *love* wherewith to feed her desolate heart; Miss Millar's cold duty was not the key that could unlock those sealed fountains.

Never, during the whole six years she was with her aunt, was her voice *heard* in song, and yet, as she afterwards told Belle, she would go away off into the woods and sing and talk too, imagining her mother's spirit could hear her.

We have dwelt thus long upon our poor Essie, because we wished our readers to understand exactly what kind of a being she was when our young friends first met her.

Of the other two children, little need be said; they were round, fat, and rosy, and a good deal indulged; their mother was very fond and very proud of them.

She tried to be good to Essie, but it was very difficult for her to conceal her aversion to her. Mr. Millar took to himself this wife, after his first had been dead one year. Her children were now five and four years old. The death of the maiden aunt, of whom we have spoken, obliged Mr. Millar to take to his own home his unloved, miserable child.

And now, as our merry party have arrived, we will let all act and speak for themselves.

CHAPTER VII.

COUNTRY LIFE.

"HERE they are! here they are! just driving through the big gate; run, Abby, run and welcome them!" said good old Nursey to her daughter.

"I wonder where Jemmy and Tommy are? do, ma, see if they look decent, while I run out to meet them."

"And Essie, Abby, where is she? Poor child, may be she'll find somebody she can fancy among the pretty little gals. Where is she, Abby?"

"O, I don't know! I guess she is up stairs poring over some book or other; never mind her, find the chicks and I'll be off." And away she ran to open the little gate and welcome the party.

Soon they were all safely ensconced in that large, old-fashioned dining-room; and Polly, the black girl, was making preparations in the kitchen for a most substantial meal. The little girls were ravenously hungry after their day's ride; and the piles of smoking brown bread, and the savory smell of doughnuts and Indian pudding, which were going upon the table, quite made their mouths water!

"Wall, wall, Lilly dear! now how you do grow, for sartain,—why, let me see, you are only seven, are ye?"

"Yes, Nursey, seven and a half, that is quite old, I think," said Lilly, straightening herself up and looking at Lena, who was about three years younger.

"Well, you *are* grown surprisin', but you a' n't quite a woman *yet*, my little darling! But who is this little one, with her great black eyes; come here and give me a kiss, won't ye, pretty one?"

Lena hung her head and clung to Lilly, for she was very timid; and the idea of kissing this old, loud-talking woman, with hardly any teeth and such a brown skin, frightened her.

"Go, Lena, go!" said Lilly. "Nursey is real good; you need n't be afraid of her if she does look queer and talk loud, she won't hurt you."

But Lena still drew back.

"Well, never mind, don't make her; you come, Lilly, and Belle, too, and kiss your old nurse and tell her you are glad to see her as she is to see you, you blessed darlings."

They did so, and Alice was then introduced, and Nurse bade her welcome.

Mr. Mordaunt and Mr. Harley now came in, and old Nurse was more than joyful at the sight again of her own child, as she called Mr. Mordaunt. Mr. Harley, too, was a great favorite of hers, although she had not seen him very often.

After a few moments, Mrs. Millar entered with a child holding each hand; they drew back rather bashfully at first, but Lilly and Belle ran to them and each took one.

Little Jennie was a fat, round, red and white little girl, with large blue eyes and wavy yellow hair; Tommy was after the same pattern, only larger, and hair darker. They were soon very much at home with the girls, and admiring eagerly the pretty things adorning their neck and arms.

How happy and bright they all looked! how full of anticipations of pleasure was each little heart! Even Alice Edmonds's eye sparkled, and a faint glow suffused her cheek as she surveyed the group, and then looked around her at the quaint old room and out of the window, where she could see a beautiful grove in the distance, and a fine lawn dotted with trees in front of the house.

"Supper is ready!" screamed Polly, very loud, for she could hardly make herself heard, there was so much talking and noise.

"O, I am so glad," said Lilly, "for I am most starved!" And I, and I, chimed in most of the others.

"Well, come along, chicks, and eat your fill, and I hope you will like it. My boy," she said, addressing Mr. Mordaunt, "won't you sit next to me? it is so long since I have seen you it does my old eyes good."

Her daughter did the honors, as Nurse considered herself too old to pour out tea any longer. At length all were seated.

"Why, here is a vacant chair by me!" said Belle; "who is to come here?"

"O, that is Essie's place," answered Nurse. "Abby, where is that child?"

"I could not prevail upon her to come down, mother! she said she did n't want to see anybody, that she *hated* girls and boys, too, and wished to be let alone and read her book."

"O, dear me, what a strange critter she is! did n't she want her tea? for I would not send it up to her and so encourage her to act so."

"No! she said she did n't, for I told her unless she would come for it she might go without."

Belle listened with much interest to this low conversation, while most of the others were busy eating and talking.

"Who is it, Nursey?" at last she said, "what little girl is so unsocial, or bashful?"

"No one you will care for, Miss Belle," said Mrs. Millar; "it is my husband's oldest child, poor Essie."

"Why is she 'poor Essie?'" still persisted Belle.

"Everybody calls her poor little Essie," said

Nurse, "because she is so crooked and small and poor, she is,— and to be pitied, I am sure,— so ugly and so strange!"

"Poor, poor little thing," said Belle, sadly; "how I wish I could see her and try to make her love me!"

"O, as to that," said Mrs. Millar, "you will see her soon enough, but you will never make her love you; for she has been with us a year now, and I am sure we have done all we could for her, and she does not love one in the house, and I sometimes feel as if she hated *me*."

"What is all this?" cried Mr. Mordaunt, who had just caught the last expression; "who are you talking about, *hating you?* Whoever it is must have very bad taste, in my opinion." And he bowed politely to Mrs. Millar.

"O, it is *only* poor Essie we were speaking of!"

"The little deformed girl of your husband?"

"Yes! have you seen her?"

"Once," said Mr. Mordaunt; "I knew her *own mother*, and spent a day there when she was living. I never saw such devotion in my life as existed between the pair during the whole day; that child never left her mother's side, — she anticipated her wishes, understood every look as well as if she were fifteen instead of five, and then, such a voice! I never heard the like in a child of her age. Even to hear her speak was a pleasure, but to hear her sing was a real delight!"

"Sing, sing!" said Mrs. Millar, "you must be mistaken. I never heard a note from her in my life, and her father never spoke of her singing; but her voice, for speaking, is rather soft and sweet."

Belle had by this time finished her supper, and while they were all busy talking she quietly slipped away, determined to seek the object of discussion; and finding the way up stairs ran into every room to hunt for her.

At last, away up in the attic, all crouched up in a heap on the floor near a window, Belle spied out the little desolate creature, who was very busy over a book, and did not hear Belle's footsteps, so that the large tears which fell so plentifully down her face upon the page were not restrained; that face was bent over, and her beautiful hair almost hid it. Belle stood still a moment, fearing to approach. While she hesitated, a low, sweet voice broke the stillness, "O, my mother! my own, own mother! why did you go and leave your child? why did you not pray to that God, who took you, to take me also? what good can I do here? everybody shuns me and I hate everybody. O mother, mother! take me to yourself." Then she hid her face upon her book and lap, and sobbed convulsively.

All at once she felt a soft arm around her neck, a warm tear drop upon her hand, and the words, "Essie, dear Essie, I love you! won't you love me a little?" uttered in such sweet, gentle tones, that Essie felt for a moment as if her prayer was answered, as if, indeed, her own mother had come to her once more, for she did not know any one else to love her. She started up and saw in the now dim light a pure, spiritual-looking creature all in white, so etherial, as it seemed to her fancy, that another idea flashed across her mind and she stood looking wildly at her; her large eyes dilated to their full extent, hardly daring to stir lest the vision should fade away, even as she gazed.

"Are you an angel, beautiful one," she said, softly, "come to take me to my mother? O, say yes, and take me! take me right away!" And she fell, trembling with excitement, at her feet.

Belle got down beside her, soothed her and caressed her, saying, "I am no angel, Essie dear, but Belle Harley, a little girl like yourself; and I have come to love you and to try to make you love me and not hate me any more, as you say you do."

"*I* said I hated *you!* how could I hate *you?* I only hate little girls and children. You are not like *them*, any that I have seen; *you* are like those pictures that mother used to show me of angels and cherubs. Your eyes are full of love, just as mother's used to be whenever she looked at me. The little girls that I have seen run away from me and call me names, and even the grown folks don't like to have me come too near. Why do you love me? say, where did you come from?"

"1 came from Boston with Lilly and Alice

and Lena, and they are all down stairs eating supper, and I came for you, dear Essie, to go down with me and eat some of the nice things. So don't sit here any longer in the dark, but come."

"No, no!" said Essie, sharply, "no! I don't want to go among all those girls. Lilly is beautiful, Mrs. Millar said so this morning, and likes to dress fine. She, I am sure, will not want the ugly little dwarf near her, and she will not like me; no one does *now*." And she sighed deeply as she pressed her book to her heart.

"O, but *they will love* you, and they are not bad girls! do come, Essie, and see if they won't, — at any rate, they won't do you any harm, and I want you to have some supper."

"I don't want any supper. I had rather read my hymn-book that mother and I used to read together."

"And didn't you sing, too?" eagerly asked Belle.

"What makes you ask me? I don't sing!"

"But you used to sing with your dear mother, didn't you? My uncle heard you once;

he used to know and love your mother, and he spent the day with her a short time before she died."

"Was that gentleman your uncle? I remember him; he was very good to me and took me on his knee, and did not seem to dislike me, as almost all strangers did; and he was very gentle to mother; I love him, and if he is there I will go down."

So they went down together, and hand in hand went into the room.

They had left the table and it was partly cleared, but Essie cared not for that, she did not wish any supper; but Mrs. Millar supposed she had come in now to get that, so she spoke quite loudly and harshly, —

"So you got Essie to come at last, did you, Miss Belle? She ought to be ashamed of herself to need so much running after; sit down now, child, and make haste."

"I don't want any supper, ma'am."

"O, very well, I'll clear away, then!"

Every body looked up and stared at Essie, and an expression like a shudder passed over the faces of Lilly and Alice, as they gazed at the shrunken and pallid face, crooked figure, and ape-like arms, of the little creature. Lilly whispered, and poor Essie heard it, for her ears were keenly sensitive, —

"Did you ever see such an ugly object? O, Alice, I wonder if we have got to play with her!"

"Hush, hush, Lilly, she hears you! see how cross she is looking at us."

Lilly was sorry as soon as she had uttered the words, but children are often just so thoughtless without meaning to be unkind.

A fierce look shot athwart the features of Essie, but only for a second; then the same sullen, reserved gloom came back again.

Mr. Mordaunt called her to him, and kindly drew her up to his side, and said, —

"Why, my little Essie, you have changed greatly since I saw you last, seven years ago; then your face was quite rosy and round, and you looked happy; poor, poor, child, you have missed your mother."

Essie could speak no word, it was only by a tremendous effort she kept from sobbing aloud; she kept clasped tightly the hand that held hers, and after a moment raised it to her lips; then she turned away with her usual look upon her face.

Mr. Harley had watched, silently, all Belle's actions, had seen her leave the table, and afterwards return with the "poor little Essie." How his heart rejoiced to see how much love and goodness there was in his sweet daughter! when his eye caught hers he gave a glance of approval, a smile of affection, and soon he motioned the pair to come to him.

Essie was about quitting the room, for she longed to be alone again, but Belle seized her hand, and dragged rather than led her unwilling captive. "I know you will love my father, Essie; so do come, he wants to see you."

Mr. Harley took one on each side of him, and put an arm around each and talked quietly and pleasantly, interesting Essie so much, that she quite forgot to think of herself, and answered and asked questions with a good deal of animation; the usual sullen look gave place to one of eager intelligence, and it was astonishing to note what a change it made in her.

Mr. Mordaunt now came up and joined the group, and seating himself by the side of Essie said, "And now, Essie, wont you sing for us? I have been telling them all how beautifully you used to sing; I hope you have not lost your voice!"

"I never sing now, except in the woods, far away from every one but mother; I don't like to sing to others, and I can't."

"O, Essie, dear, won't you sing one song to me? I should so love to hear you."

"And I, and I," shouted a number of voices, for they had already gotten over their dread of her first appearance, and, child-like, were eager to hear something new.

"Not now, indeed I can't now, but some other time I will sing for you, Mr. Mordaunt, for (she added in a whisper) you loved my dear mother."

"Yes, indeed, I did, little Essie, we grew up together here in this village, and Hester Gray was the village beauty; we played together and went to school together, and I loved her as if she were my own sister."

Essie drew closer to him, and pressed another kiss upon his hand.

"Poor child, poor child!" said he, "to lose such a mother was hard for thee. Essie," he added, after a pause, "I leave early to-morrow morning, and this is the only chance I shall have to hear you sing."

"Do you really want to hear me so much?"

"Why, yes, child! of course I do."

"Well, I must then, if I can."

So taking a low seat in front of him, with her back to all the rest, she began that beautiful song, "My Mother Dear!"

At first the tones were tremulous and low, but soon she forgot all but her song, and her voice poured out so rich, so clear, and musical, that all stared, mute with admiration and surprise. Even Mrs. Millar stood stock-still in the midst of her dish-washing, with a cup between her fingers, and her eyes very wide open gazing in wonder towards the form from whence those heavenly words proceeded; and old Nurse forgot to knit, and sat looking up with the stocking resting in her lap.

When the last faint tones — "My mother dear!" — died upon the ear, almost every eye in the room was moistened; every heart beat faster, throbbing with emotion.

There were no cruel, unkind ones there; only an insensibility, a bluntness of nature, which prevented their understanding or appreciating such a character as Essie's. This caused their apparent unfeelingness, and Essie's dislike.

This song seemed to unlock all hearts, and good-natured Abby Millar thought, "Well, there may be something in the strange child, after all!"

Before any one could collect themselves to speak, Essie had slipped away.

"By Jove!" said Mr. Mordaunt, who was the first to break the pause (and who, although a very kind-hearted man, was often inelegant in his expressions); "by Jove, what a voice! did you ever hear as much soul put into a song before? why, if that girl had a person to match her voice she might make her fortune in a few years. Mrs. Millar," he added, turning to her, "that is no common girl; be careful of her, — she feels every word, every look."

"Yes," said Mr. Harley, gently, "hers is a spirit that must be very tenderly dealt with; nothing but love and kindness should ever meet her ear."

"I guess she can't complain of her treatment here," said Mrs. Millar, bridling up; "she has always had everything she wanted, and, if I knew how, I would have made her happy; but she hates me, I think, and I always fancied it was because I took her mother's place; but then, she don't seem to love her father much, either."

The gentlemen were silent. They saw there was no use talking to Mrs. Millar; she was too well satisfied with herself, and had too little penetration to read such a character as Essie's. So, to change the subject, Mr. Harley inquired after Mr. Millar.

"O, he has gone away for a month or so to look after some land of his out West! Perhaps we shall all go and live there when he comes back."

The children, Lilly and Lena, came up and told their father they were going to play blindman's buff. Several of the neighbors' children had come in, and there was to be a fine game.

Mr. Harley and Mr. Mordaunt betook themselves to another room, and read the papers and talked. After awhile, however, the merry sounds in the adjoining apartment tempted them and they went back too look on, and even join in the game. Mrs. Millar, and old Nurse, too, helped on the fun, and a right pleasant evening they had.

Belle made her escape in the midst of the jollity and ran off again to hunt up her new little friend, in whom she felt so interested that she could not bear to leave her alone. Her own heart sympathised so keenly with the afflicted child's sufferings, that she longed to make her happy, to be her comforter. The sorrowful tones she first heard from her sounded in her ears in the midst of all the fun; and her desolate, despairing attitude was continually before her eyes, even when she had the blinder on and was apparently very gay.

She found her in her own little room, and, as usual, she was weeping over her mother's hymn-book.

Belle stole gently up behind her and put her arms around her neck, and said, "I have left the play, dear Essie, for I longed to be with you, and I knew I should not be missed, there are so many there."

Essie looked up, and something of a loving expression came into her face, as she met those soft, sweet eyes bent upon her so affectionately.

"Why do you come after me?" she said; "leave me to my loneliness, no one can care for such as I am but one, and she is in heaven."

"Essie, do you refuse to let me love you? do you want me to go away? does it make you more unhappy to have me near you, and to have me try to make you love me?"

Essie looked up, and upon her features again shone that beautiful look of grateful love, and yet she could not speak; but Belle saw the look, and pressing her hand gently, said again, "I may stay here, Essie dear?"

"May? and do you, then, really want to be with *me*, — *me*, the poor despised dwarf? and do you think I would not love to have you?

O Belle! dear, dear Belle! if you only knew how I pined and longed for love, how one loving word comes like balm to my aching heart, you would not ask such a question."

"But you did not seem to want me, darling; your words were harsh, and your tone cold."

"Was I? Ah, well, I could not believe in the dream which the first sound of your voice sent to my heart. I feared to admit any one into my secret thoughts. I suspected you and feared to love you, thinking I could never win your love; but, Belle, I cannot look into your face and doubt anything; all suspicions flee, and I must love you!"

Belle seated herself beside her, and the two young girls were for that hour, at least, happy together.

After this Belle and Essie were constantly together. Belle succeeded in winning her love, because she had the right key to her heart. Not too little, but too much feeling, too keen sensibilities, had made the child draw into herself and seem indifferent to all things. A shudder, a tone, a look, were all noticed by her, and cut like daggers into her heart, which was just as sensitive also to real kindness, and sympathy, and love.

The little party in the dining-room, which we left to follow Belle and Essie, after having a royal time, eat some nuts and apples, and then separated to retire.

Belle, when she heard all quiet, hastened down to say good night to the little neighbors, and also to her father and uncle. Then the little folks all went quietly to bed.

Belle and Alice slept together, and Lilly and Lena. Essie had a little room to herself, which was a great comfort to her at night, for no other part of the day could she be free from interruption in it, as Mrs. Millar kept the children's clothes here, and used it also for a sewing-room and a nursery.

Mr. Harley and Mr. Mordaunt left the next day, with many cautions to the older ones to take care of the others, and also, all of them to be as little troublesome as possible; Mrs. Mordaunt was to come to them in a week or two, as soon as the friends who were with her left. Alice talked to Belle a long while about her new *protégé,* as she called her, and laughed somewhat at the sudden fancy which seemed to inspire her for one so uncouth and apparently unamiable.

"Alice," said Belle, "do not talk in that heartless manner, I cannot hear you; have you no compassion for misfortune and sorrow? Place yourself in her situation, what would you like others to do to you, avoid and hate you? look on you with pity, but loathing, and leave you to loneliness and grief?" Belle spoke very earnestly, almost sharply for her, and Alice's bad passions were called into play, for the lion was not yet tamed in her heart; and to tell the truth, she was rather jealous of the hold this stranger seemed to have taken upon Belle's affections.

"Well Belle, really you need not take one up quite so sharply; I don't know as there is any particular reason why you should cut your old friends, leave them altogether, and be cold and cross to them, merely to defend this new comer."

"Cross! was I, Alice? I am sure I did not mean to be; and O, dear Alice, you know I never desert my old friends, you know how much I love you; surely, Alice, after all our pleasant hours passed together, you cannot doubt it; I left you all enjoying, yourselves and full of glee, I knew none of you would miss me, and I could not bear to think of that poor, pale, sad looking little thing being all alone in her grief, so I ran off to find her, and if you had been with me, Ally dear, you would not have spoken of her as you did, I know; forgive me if I spoke harshly, and let us be good friends again, won't you, deary?"

"Ah, Belle, you were not cross, it is only myself, and my own ugly spirit as it always is, that makes any trouble between us; but one cannot resist you, no one can keep cross long where you are."

"Well, now Alice, if we are friends again, promise me you will try and love Essie, and not let her see you shrink from her; promise me, do, that you will do all you can to make her happy while we are here, won't you now, Ally dear?"

"Yes, yes I will, but she will not care much for any of us as long as she can have you;

but I hope she will like me a little too, for if she don't, I see clearly I shall never have any of your society except at night, so I shall make friends with her, if I can, that we can all be together."

Before a week passed away, Essie's love was completely won by Belle, and the affection which beamed from her large brown eyes, whenever she looked upon her, almost made her face for the moment beautiful.

The children all had gotten over their first fear of her, and no longer shrank from the touch of her long arms, or gazed with horror at her hump and short figure; she kept somewhat aloof from them all, however, so they had not much in common. Alice fulfilled her promise, and was really kind and amiable to her; but Essie's was a reserved nature, and her confidence did not flow forth easily, so she was always silent in Alice's company. Belle was constantly trying to infuse into her heart some of her own beautiful love and trust in people.

One bright, pleasant day, about three weeks after their arrival, they were returning from an exploring expedition to some woods, about a mile or so from the house. Belle, Essie, and Alice, were together; Essie was more gay than she was ever wont to be. "What a lovely walk we have had," she said, and her face looked so joyous that she seemed like another being from the one of our first acquaintance.

"Yes, we have indeed," said both the girls, in a breath; "but now," said Alice, "I must run back and join Lilly and Lena, for I am afraid they are far from us and will lose their way; besides, Lilly has my wreath and my shawl, and I want them both."

"Sha'n't we all go back, then," said Belle? "I guess we had better."

"O no, Belle, I rather think Essie has walked far enough, and will be tired when she gets home."

"Yes, said Belle, true enough. I did not think of that Ally dear; you seem to have wits for us all, this afternoon!"

Alice ran off, and the two were alone. "It seems to me," said Essie, "I never feel tired when I am with you, Belle dear; O, how I love to be! How good you are to me, and why should you care for me so much? no one else ever has, or does, but my own angel mother."

"Essie," replied Belle, in her sweet, tender voice, "you are wrong in thinking no one loves you, and you are wrong in acting as if you thought so; and, dear Essie, if you will only have that love in your own heart which you would like to have cherished for you,— if you would only drop that cold reserve which keeps every one from knowing you as you are, and have trust and faith, you would be so much happier and make others so much happier."

"I make others happier! What do you suppose, Belle, it matters to those at home how I look or act? So I keep my ugly self out of the way, that is all they care for. My absence or death might make them happier, I presume!"

"Indeed, indeed Essie, you are wrong! you are so mistaken, no one feels so about you, and you would find out how wrong you were if you would only use what gifts God has given you, rightly. Now, dear Essie, you live only for yourself, and hug up your own sorrows, and will not see what you can make bright about you."

"It is easy for you to talk thus, Belle," she replied, bitterly, "with all your loveliness, your grace, your wealth, &c.; but what gifts have been bestowed upon me to call forth my gratitude? The only gift I have prayed for, and longed for, has been denied, *death*, — for what, then, have I to be grateful?"

"Essie, Essie, you are not fit to die yet. O, you know not what you ask! God in his mercy has spared you for wise and good purposes; and you will one day see and acknowledge his love in all things, even in your misfortunes, which you now speak of so bitterly."

"What, Belle, be thankful for the curse sent upon me? See love in my life of misery? I may be reconciled to it; but grateful for anything concerning my existence, I cannot be."

Belle sighed, and looked sadly at the excited girl, as she replied: "Will you let me tell you, Essie dear, what you have to be grateful for in common with us all, and some things which few have besides? First, then, for life; for is it not a pleasure to live in this beautiful world, to watch the flowers grow, to listen to the songs of birds, to look on such sights as this now around us?" They both stopped for a moment to survey the lovely landscape spread out upon all sides, gilded by the departing rays of a most gorgeous sunset. "Look! O look, Essie! are not those clouds

> "Like golden vistas into heaven"

Essie's rapt face showed she fully appreciated the beauty, and had a soul to enjoy it. "Secondly," continued Belle, after a moment's silence, "you have talents, intelligence, mind, which can afford you great delight. Thirdly, you have the gift of song, a most beautiful voice with which to gratify others, and amuse and employ yourself. Fourthly, you have the power in you of making friends, if you choose to exert it, and you might be a great blessing to all around you. Lastly, you have a good home, all your bodily wants well cared for, and people around you who mean to be kind to you, although they may not understand how.

There now, you naughty girl, I have read you a long sermon, and we are almost home; but, ere we get there, dear Essie," and she looked at her with her sweet eyes full of tenderness, " promise me you will try and get rid of your suspicion and coldness; let love enter your heart and take up its abode there; love for all, will you; say, Essie?"

Essie pressed her young teacher's hand, and with her eyes full of tears, said, " For you, dear Belle, I will try to change; for you and mother I would do everything."

From that day, there was a marked alteration in Essie. She was more gracious to all around her, stayed among others more, and often sung when asked, and sometimes joined in their games; even from Lilly she shrank less, although her exceeding beauty was such a painful contrast that the sight of her awoke more of the bitterness that still rankled in her heart.

One morning Mrs. Millar exclaimed, " What has come over Essie? she is really amusing the children; look at her with little Janey on her lap, and Tommy at her side, and one arm around him; gracious me! a fortnight or three weeks ago and she would n't touch them if she could help it; after all, she a'n't so bad looking, mother, her face now is so pleasant." Her mother's heart was touched; poor Essie had never looked pleasant in Mrs. Millar's eyes before!

"Yes," said Nursey, "and this morning she came and brought me a real pretty knitting-sheath, and laid it in my lap, never saying a word. I know what it is; that Belle is an angel, Abby; she is a blessed child, but she won't live long; look at her skin showing every vein, and then her eyes so bright and so dark around them; besides, she is ripe for heaven and no mistake!"

"Yes, yes! I think so too, mother; and yet she seems perfectly well."

Just then Belle came in, followed by Alice, Lilly, and Lena; they had all been out having a nice play in the barn and swinging, their cheeks were rosy and their eyes sparkling; so fresh and radiant was Belle that her appearance seemed to deny the assertion just made, and Nurse exclaimed:

"Country air is making you a different looking lassie; your father will hardly know you. And Miss Alice, too, she has gained ever so much."

"Yes," said Alice, "in health and happiness too. If you only knew how much good you had done me, Mrs. Randall, by admitting me as one of the children, I am sure you would not regret being a little crowded."

"No more I do, Miss Alice. Ah, it does my old eyes good to see so many of your young faces together. I hope you will feel like one of them, and come whenever they do, in future."

"Thank you! thank you! I am sure I shall wish to; but I have a new mother now that I shall have to mind, — it will be as she says."

"Well, then," said Belle, joining in the conversation, "you will come; for, as I have often told you, Alice, I know your new mother; she lived near us, and she is just as good and kind as she is pretty, and you will love her dearly."

"May be so; at any rate I shall try to, if only to please you, Belle."

"Why, how you all love Belle," said Mrs.

Millar; "I wonder the rest of you a'n't jealous, she is such a favorite."

"Jealous! jealous of Belle! that would be queer, indeed," said Lilly; "why, she ought to be loved the best, there is no one like her; who could be jealous of our Belle?" And she threw her arms around her neck and hugged and kissed her.

Alice colored, for she remembered the time when her jealousy had caused so much misery to herself and others, but she did not speak.

Essie now came forward, with a child in each hand, and said, "And so the picnic comes off to-morrow; is that what you are all talking about?"

"No, that is not what we were talking about; but it is to-morrow," said Mrs. Millar, "and won't you all have a grand time?"

"And oh!" said little Lena, scrabbling up in Nurse Randall's lap, "is n't it nice that we are going to stay here six whole weeks, or a month longer?" (All fear of the old Nurse had departed, and she was a great pet and plaything.)

"Yes, yes, my darlings, I am right glad

your time is lengthened; but sorry Lilly's mother and the baby can't get here until just before you go."

The girl's vacation was extended in consequence of the marriage of Mr. Burbank and Miss Manners. As they were not to teach any longer, the girls were going to another school. Lena's mother had also left that school, and set up a French class for herself, which was well patronized, — so Adèle was very happy. After Mrs. Burbank returned from her wedding tour, Adèle, with Lena, was to live with her; an arrangement so delightful for the affectionate, dependent little Madame, that her joy was too great for expression.

So all were pleased, the girls particularly, that they were to enjoy the lovely country until late in fall.

But among all, none were so happy as poor Essie. To have her dear Belle six weeks longer, was indeed a felicity.

The girls felt badly to lose their teachers, but thought it such a nice match. "And then poor Mr. Burbank has been teaching so long," said Belle, "he deserves to rest."

Essie's happiness was deep, but silent, since the advent of Belle into that house. Life had assumed a new aspect to that sad heart, and she began to feel that even she, with all her sorrows, had a great deal to be grateful for, and a good many to love.

CHAPTER VIII.

THE PICNIC.

THE morning arose fair and cloudless, and many hearts beat high with joyful anticipation; all the village children, boys and girls, fourteen years old and under, were invited, and many of the mothers, or older relatives were to go, to see that all went right, and to take care of the younger ones.

Belle had had great difficulty in persuading Essie to be one among them.

"O no! I never go to such things," she said, "I do not know the village children, and I hate to be where there are so many to stare at me; no one will care about it, but you Belle, and you only tease me to go, because you think I would enjoy it; but when you know I should not, when you know it will be actual pain to me, surely, dear Belle, you will urge me no more."

"No, no! I will give it up then, Essie, but half my pleasure is destroyed; and I know, too, the children, Tommy and Janey, will miss you sadly."

"And," said Alice, "what will we do without Essie to sing for us?"

"And," chimed in little Lena, "who can make such lovely wreaths as Essie, and who will spy out all the pretty flowers?"

"And," said Mrs. Millar, speaking really gently, and softly for her, "who will take care so well of my babies?"

And then Belle looked at her so imploringly with her soft brown eyes, that she relented, saying, with a pleased expression, "Well, if you all want me so much, I must go, and shall be glad to be useful!"

· · · · ·

Lilly was chosen queen, for she was so beautiful, that she had the vote of all the villagers. How proud and happy was little Lena, who was one of her maids of honor, to wait upon this, the young sovereign of a day. Belle wrote a very sweet little poetical address, which was to be spoken upon crowning her, and Essie was to sing, some time in the day, a little song also composed by Belle, called "The Woodland Party," and set to music by Essie; everything was arranged satisfactorily.

Polly and Mrs. Millar, with Essie's help, had made quantities of pies, cakes, and brown bread, and boiled ham, and lots of chickens. The old Nurse was to be there, as well as the rest; she was to ride in a wagon with the provisions and Mrs. Millar and the little ones.

The day, as I said before, dawned brightly, and at nine o'clock, forty merry souls were assembled at the old farm "Woodside," as the nearest "rendezvous."

The girls were dressed in white, with blue sashes, and the boys in white pants and roundabouts, — what a happy set they were; not a sad face, not a cross look was visible, and their glad voices rang out in merry, joyous chimes upon the soft, balmy air.

Essie kept in the back ground; she, too, was dressed in white, and her long curls never shone more glossily, or shaded her face when it looked more happy and content.

The procession formed two and two, they kept thus a short time, when the regularity was dispensed with, and groups walked together.

Lena carried the basket with the queen's wreath, and proud was she of her burden. A young lad, they called Frank, walked by Lilly's side, who seemed to be much occupied looking at her; there were a good many boys among them, and some rather mischievous ones, too, I should judge from the pranks that every little while were played off, such as trying to kiss the girls, and to make them take their arms, and, now and then, sticking stiff dandelions or weeds in their bonnets.

"Oh! oh! let me alone!" says Emma Lindon, "Bob, get out of the way, I will not take your arm. Now a'n't you ashamed, sticking Bessie Groat's bonnet full of that old everlasting?"

"Hush, hush, Emma! don't tell her, she don't know it, and don't it look, too, funny?" And it did, indeed; for Bessie was a tall, thin girl, with a high-crowned bonnet on, upon the very top of which Bob had contrived to fasten a great bunch of everlasting, making it stand straight up. They both laughed, and Emma kept still.

The next thing he tried, was to teaze Lena, by pulling at the precious wreath, or pretending to; Lena fled to Belle for protection. Then his mischievous eyes spied out Essie.

"O," he whispers to Emma, "here is little humpy, I'll fix her up now."

"Come, Tom, you go pick that great big dockleaf, and yonder is a dahlia, she shall have a feather in her cap soon."

Tom, like most boys, was up to the fun, and went. Bob tied the leaf and the flower together, and crept softly up behind Essie, and while she and Belle were very busy talking, tucked it in the ribbon of her hat. Whereupon, many of the children set up a shout, and if "poor Essie" had known how ridiculous she looked, she would have been most deeply pained, for she was so sensitive to ridicule.

Before, however, she could understand what all the shouting and laughter was about, Alice had stepped quickly up to her, and snatched the thing out, then looking haughtily at the boy, said, "I am sorry you have so little feeling, or sense, either."

Alice had not yet learned to be gentle in her reproofs; her indignation or anger aroused, would come forth in words and looks.

The boy was hurt; he did not mean to be ugly, he only wanted a little fun, and was thoughtless as boys usually are who have not been taught as a constant and daily practice the beautiful rule which our sweet Belle so loved. His face crimsoned, and he darted an angry look at Alice.

Belle turned around at the instant, saw the look, and thought to herself that it would never do to have clouds arising so early in the day. So she said : —

"Ally dear, do come here, won't you? and Bob, too, and Tom. We want you large folks all to hurry forward and see if the bower is ready, and all right; if not, use your taste in finishing it up."

"Will you come too, Belle?" said Alice; you have more taste than any of us."

"Yes, I'll go and leave Essie with Lilly, Lena, and the rest, while we run on."

And on they hastened, all ill-feeling gone and forgotten. . . . . . .

"What a lovely bower! O, did you ever see anything so perfect?" said Alice; "who built it?"

"Essie, and Frank, and I," said Belle, "but Essie planned it."

"What, that little dwarf with the cross face that I have seen lately at the old farm, and who is with us to-day?" said Bob and Tom in a breath.

"O, boys don't speak of her in that way! don't! I am sure you would not hurt her feelings if you knew her, you could not be so rude as well as unkind."

"Well, Belle," replied Tom, "I will be more careful, but I thought none of the folks liked her over there, and that she was sullen and cross."

Well, and if she were so, which is not true, suppose you were afflicted as she is, a painful object for all eyes to gaze upon and shudder, would you be very amiable or sociable, do you think? But Essie only needs love and tenderness to draw her thoughts from herself, and then she is more lovable than most of us, and her talents are remarkable; but she is sensitive beyond measure, and particularly so to ridicule."

Bob was listening attentively to all Belle said, and he blushed with shame in thinking of his last exploit; but he determined in his own mind to make up for it by peculiar kindness to her the rest of the day.

And now all the children and all the party were fairly assembled in those lovely woods, and what a glorious day was it for those happy young hearts, — nothing interfered to mar the pleasure, after the little scene on the way there. Lilly looked beautifully, blushing and modest, when she knelt before Frank Morris to receive her crown of flowers, and still more lovely was her bright face when she arose with the rosebuds and lilies for a coronal. Lena and three other little girls of the same age were the maids of honor, and never did the hearts of any real attendant upon a real sovereign beat with more importance than the hearts of these five-year-old maidens.

The queen was not too dignified to mingle

in the sport. She was even seen playing "tag," "king's ground," and also swinging as gaily and noisily as her subjects; and one part of the day (ah! tell it not in Gath) she might have been observed with her pretty white feet bare, her pantalets rolled up, wading in the clear running brook, her maids of honor all in her train, as well as a number of other little girls. . . . . . What a dinner that was; spread out upon the white cloth on a smooth green place, overshadowed by large, closely intertwined trees.

The queen was served first by the king, then each in order helped themselves. How hungry everybody felt, and how good everything tasted, and how delighted were the older people to see so many happy faces around.

About an hour after dinner all assembled together to hear some music; there were several sweet singers among them, and the band were allowed to sit in the bower, the rest clustered around to listen.

Song after song followed in quick succession, but now the queen called for a solo from Essie!

What a buzz of astonishment rose up from many who did not know she could sing at all, who had never thought of poor Essie as able to do anything like other people.

This was a hard trial for our little Essie to get up and sing there before so many who cared not for her, and that she did not wish to please; but she had promised her dear Belle, and go through it she would, if possible.

At first, her voice trembled very perceptibly, but ere the six or eight stanzas were completed, it swelled forth gloriously. It commenced thus: —

> "Come all ye that love joy and pleasure,
>   Come join in our frolic to-day;
> We will have mirth and sport without measure,
>   Each heart and each face must be gay.
>
> "Our queen is a sweet little creature,
>   As all who look once will say;
> Our king, too, all grant, is a treasure,
>   E'en worthy the queen to obey."

Then followed a description of many of the girls, and it ended with a hope that all might meet again in the lovely woodland grove; but if not to meet ever in this world, then

"In that beautiful heaven where all is bright,
Where sorrow ne'er enters, nor pain, nor night,
May we meet and love on, for aye."

The last strains died away so beautifully soft and clear, so full of pathos were the tones, that every heart was touched, and many eyes moistened with tears.

The poetry for a girl of eleven, was quite creditable, and at any rate, at that time, all thought it beautiful ; probably Essie's lovely voice aided the effect. There was not a heart there that did not warm towards the poor desolate one, upon hearing those heavenly tones.

The singing over, the whole party joined in a round of merry games, and then their elders proclaimed it was time to prepare for home ; and, after various detentions, from hunting up stray articles and stray children, the party started.

For about a half a mile, all walked together ; then came good byes and affectionate leave-takings, and before long, the little company from "Woodside" were alone.

Essie, with the two children, for they had

begged to walk home with sissy, of whom lately they had become very fond, walked with Belle and Alice. Lilly and Lena, with the young king, who would not leave his queen until the last minute, were also together.

It was a beautiful evening, the sun just setting clearly, while a rosy, hazy light, was over all the landscape; the woods, behind them, stood out boldly against the sky, and the pretty village, with its picturesque spires, was bathed in the departing glory.

The girls lingered to enjoy the hour, so that Lilly, and Lena, and Frank, were soon out of sight. They were standing still, gazing and admiring; "How lovely the pond looks," exclaimed Alice, "so lighted up by the sun, and see the bright flowers all around the bank! Surely they were never there before."

"O," said Essie, "I have robbed its margin often this summer; but they do show more sweetly than ever before, it seems to me."

"Sissy, I want one of those pretty flowers," said Tommy, "and I mean to get some, too; so away he ran as quick as thought to the pond, no one dreaming of any danger.

He stooped down, and reached over for the brightest looking flower, it was a little beyond his reach, but he leaned still farther, lost his balance, and fell headlong into the water.

Essie had already started for the boy when she saw him fall, then with a scream of anguish almost heart-rending, she darted to the spot, but he had disappeared beneath the thick dark water; instantly he rose again, some distance from the bank; without a single thought of self, Essie plunged in, and succeeded in jumping near enough to the place where he appeared, to reach him with one of her long arms; with the other, she had clutched hold of a long branch of a tree which grew on the bank and overshadowed the pond, this one hanging far down, and far out from the land. The girls were there in a moment; there was the brave child, with Tommy a perfectly dead weight in one arm, and the other holding on with might and main to the tree; her face was very, very pale, and she was gasping with her efforts, but she must keep Tommy's head above water, and her own, too; what could be done? they could not reach her, and she surely could not hold on long enough for one to run to the house for assistance; what agony unspeakable was concentrated in these few minutes. But one had already started for the house; it was Belle; she almost flew. Alice remained to cheer and encourage the fainting Essie.

What an age it seemed; Essie's cheek grew more and more ghastly, the arm which held Tommy relaxed, only his head was above water, her own head sunk lower; "alas, alas, she will sink, she will die! what shall I do, what shall I do?" And Alice wrung her hands in despair.

Just as all hope was about departing from both, Alice espied Farmer Hazlewood, running, with Belle after him, and others from the farm.

"Hold on, hold on, Essie dear, they are here; one moment, and you are safe, keep up!"

Hope inspired her with fresh strength, and she kept up.

They were soon rescued from their perilous situation by the strong man, but Essie sank lifeless into his arms. He walked the short distance, for the water was not over his head,

— about up to his shoulders,— and held one in each arm. Tommy he placed in his mother's care, (for she had rushed to the spot, and was almost frantic with terror,) Essie he laid upon the bank until he came up, and then he carried her to the house. It was a mournful procession home, how different from the bright scene of the morning; every voice was hushed and every heart was sad, for none knew as yet the extent of the mischief, they both lay so pale and lifeless.

Little Tommy soon came to himself, upon rubbing, and looked around him in a sort of amazed way; he had been more frightened than hurt; poor Mrs. Millar, however, thought she had lost her darling, and when he opened his blue round eyes and gazed at her, she clasped him to her heart with a fervent ejaculation of joy.

With Essie it was a far more serious adventure; it was amazing how such a little frail creature could have exerted so much strength, for at other times she could scarce lift Tommy from the floor into her lap; he was a great stout boy of five.

She was laid upon the bed, and everything done to restore animation, but for a long time all means failed, and one looked at the other with sad tearful eyes, while hope was dying in their hearts; at length, however, her large dreamy eyes unclosed and fixed upon Mrs. Millar who was bending anxiously over her.

"Where am I?" she asked, in the lowest whisper. "I have had such a dream! I thought little Tommy was drowned, and that it was my fault; and then I thought I was drowned too, and went to Heaven; and O how happy I was, mother was so glad to see me. But here I am, and here you all are! But where is Tommy, say, is he safe?"

"He is, Essie dear, safe, and you saved him, and you are my blessed child. O Essie, forgive me, forgive me, for all my hardness, for my blindness, and love me a little!" And the tears rained upon her cheeks.

"Forgive you! O, God be thanked, I have then found another mother, — another who will love me like a child! Mother! I love to say that word. Mother, I will live for you and father now; I hope I no longer wish to die!"

But now that Essie was resigned to live, aye, even happy in the prospect of life, she was to be taken from all who loved her; she had remained long enough to be fitted for death, and now, amidst regret and unavailing sorrow, she was to be wafted to that heaven she so loved.

Yet still she lingered long! That sick room was a holy and beautiful lesson to all who entered it. All summer she remained among them, gradually growing weaker and paler; the shock and the chill was too great for her sickly frame, and she died in saving another, happy, too, in such a death.

Poor Mrs. Millar! bitterly did her heart reproach her for all her wrong to that suffering child; ah, how gladly would she have toiled for her through life, could she but be spared to her now. For weeks, Mrs. Millar's eyes had been opening to the good in Essie, and her heart softening towards her, and often had doubts crept into her mind as to whether she had always been as kind and gentle as she ought to be towards the poor child; and now this last act of self-devotion completely subduced the (really not hard) heart of the stepmother; she loved her truly and deeply, and longed for her to live in order that she might atone for past injustice.

Mr. Millar, Essie's father, came home and found his neglected child dying; then awoke the father's heart within him, then the earnest appeals of his lost wife for his poor girl came to his mind like dagger-strokes, causing him to writhe with anguish!

"O, my poor abused child," he cried, "live, live for your father, that he may show you now, how he loves you."

Essie would look so deeply, purely happy, when so much love fell upon her ear; her sweet low voice would come to him with comforting words, and she would wind her arms around his neck and kiss him so tenderly.

"It was all my own fault, father, and mother, too, it was all my fault, you did not know me, I was sullen and cross, and hated everybody; then there was no love in my own heart, and I deserved none. It was dear Belle that taught me how bad I was, and since she showed me the way to love people, I have been so much happier!"

Thus she talked and soothed those in trouble around her. The girls all wanted to be near her; but they took turns at her bedside, Belle's turn coming oftenest, — for the dying child could hardly bear her out of her sight.

The night before she died, one of her long beautiful curls was cut off for each of her dearest friends.

She died in Belle's arms, with her father, mother, and grandmother around the bed; her father wiping the death-dew from her pale forehead, her last look was upon him; her last words were, "mother dearest, I come! God bless you all. We shall meet above." Tranquilly, serenely, and painlessly, she departed to her home in the sky.

Every attention and care had been bestowed upon her, the best of physicians and the tenderest of nurses always near, but naught availed; she was prepared for her home on high, and to it God in his love had taken her.

· · · · ·

Poor Essie never was forgotten by any one

who knew her that summer. The girls, with their parents, left the village soon after her burial, and returned to Boston.

Should any of our young readers desire to hear more about them, they may, perhaps, at some future time.

THE END.

www.ingramcontent.com/pod-product-compliance
Lightning Source LLC
Chambersburg PA
CBHW020252170426
43202CB00008B/330